WOLVES LIKE US

The Wolfland Trilogy

Part 1

press twenty-one

Wolf logo by PGDC

ISBN 978-3-9817419-7-1

Digitally printed in Australia, the United States and the United Kingdom

Randolph, Natascha and Philip
Rachel; Meike; Golo
Niklas and Alix; Charlie
Jacob and Josephine

Contents

As she turned towards me and got closer I looked right into her eyes: Brown-black eyes, wolf eyes, beautiful-brown-black-Xola-wolf-eyes, looking at me out of a lovely face with an oriental touch that I had tried so hard to refuse to remember and yet had been unable to forget.

Xola

Day 1
I was spellbound, completely knocked off my feet, the very instant I set eyes on her.

Sometimes there are these moments in life when half an eternity gets rolled into a split second. Just one of these eternities ago we were stumbling through the deep snow, heading towards where we thought we might find shelter from the icy wind and the cold that was draining the last bits of energy from our bodies. Shadowy shapes were milling around us as if coaxing us on in a distinct direction. Every now and then the wind would tear apart a cloud of drifting snow and the silhouettes turned into shadows of bodies, wolves' bodies, parts thereof, heads with gleaming eyes, furry bodies. Then we ran almost smack-dead into the embankment, rising sharply out of the pitch-dark arctic nothingness. As we struggled upwards, it stood there right in front of us, out of nowhere, hoped and prayed for and yet at that very moment totally unexpected: The cabin, an ex-fur trapper's log cabin.

Perhaps I should tell things from the beginning. We were ferrying a DeHavilland Beaver from Camp Bravo back to base, to be retired from active service and then, perhaps, sold off to some vintage aircraft enthusiast, broken up to be sold for scrap or sent to an aviation museum, whatever the financial geniuses at head office considered most appropriate. Although still widely used throughout Canada and Alaska, ours was a very early model and had been in storage for several years, stashed away in a hangar gathering dust. Then someone had remembered it and it was important to get it back to base as soon as possible: ASAP was pointed out emphatically.

The flight had the makings of what in the industry is commonly referred to as a milk-run, the least ambitious form of commercial or military flying imaginable, no secret mission, no hidden agenda, no covert objective, no passengers or cargo or otherwise; just to get from A to B in one piece. On that day I had a lot going through my head. First thing in the morning I found a memo from Emerson, personal assistant to the CEO, informing me that they wanted to post me to one of the newly acquired oilfields of the Company in Venezuela, which would collide diametrically with some personal plans of mine. And as if that wasn't enough personnel sent me a note: I was to be promoted from active flying to administering the Caribbean operation, based in Caracas. There must have been a conspiracy behind my back. Quite obviously somebody wanted to do me in. Everybody in the company knew that I would turn down an admin assignment with no active flying duties.

I was not exactly in a brilliant mood when I got down to the flight line, but it improved exponentially as soon as I caught sight of the Beaver, being readied for flight outside the one and only proper sized hangar at Camp Bravo that was mostly used for storing things that we didn't need any more.

I had been looking forward to this trip - could not really explain my passion for flying the Beaver. It was just not run-of-the-mill-stuff, something special, promising to become a fun trip, something that does not challenge your skills and abilities yet gives you enough opportunities to enjoy the exhilarating feeling of controlled flight, man, machine and the elements, experiencing what flying is all about.

We were quite casual and relaxed. I flew the aircraft and Harry was in the right-hand seat of the cockpit. He had come along for the ride, to report to base for a new assignment. Harry was a self-improved helicopter pilot who had turned from amateur enthusiast to commercial aviator via a succession of courses, schools and junior jobs with better known to obscure companies. He sometimes jokingly referred to himself as a 'failed trapeze artist'. Rumour had it that he had been a stockbroker on Wall Street and weekend amateur helicopter pilot, until one day, maybe it was on Black Friday, he pushed the wrong button, issuing computerised instructions to sell, say, half a million pigs' halves or something like that, when the market was really low, whereupon he got a summons to the boss's office the next Monday morning, 'a letter of recommendation' and a strongly worded suggestion to contemplate a career change: he was fired.

He went for some more professional pilot training and started working his way west, until he wound up with the Karibak Pipeline Company in Alaska, where he had been ferrying supplies and people into and out of the field for most of last year. Field was a colloquial reference in our company lingo for the rest of the world, everything outside the base perimeter fence.

To stave off boredom Harry had asked me to give him something useful to do during the flight that would take a little over three hours. So, I let him do what is called the flight-following and work the radio to call in our position, strictly a one-way business, just letting them know. As the pilot I had prepared and filed a flight plan. It was a succession of three straight lines, linked by two-way points. Easy! All we had to do was make sure we were on track. Navigation would be child's play. Just fly straight, compensate a little for crosswind, one right turn, one left and you were home.

Yes! Home! I was flying home! How I had been looking forward to it; home in successive stages, first to Base, then on to England or rather the UK, my country of citizenship. Earlier in the morning I had been to see Al Hickman as he was putting the finishing touches to readying the Beaver for the flight.

"Eh . . . she check out OK, Al?" I asked him.

"Sure does. She's a fine little bird, my pride and joy." Al beamed at me and he certainly meant every word of it. People said the inside of his house usually looked like shit but the hangar, his tools and especially the aircraft he worked on always were in mint condition. He was an aviator to the core and probably had kerosene or aviation gasoline pulsing through his veins.

"What's her maintenance status and condition?" From – bad – experience I always got a little edgy when someone said something that implied 'no problem'. I wanted to know the bottom line. If there was anything, I needed to know this would be one of the better moments to tell me.

"Last time she came in here she was about two hundred and fifty hours out of a major overhaul and an engine and propeller change. Since then she's only done another forty-eight hours in the air." Al gave me a broad grin.

"In two years?" I was concerned. As with cars and most other technical equipment aircraft do not like to be parked for long periods of time. The one thing every aviator fears like the plague is corrosion, the invisible enemy that can eat your aircraft up from inside without you ever seeing it.

"We've been running the engine for about half an hour once a week. That should have made sure that all systems got proper lubrication and kept out corrosion." He put out his right hand, in which he held a clipboard with a technical status report on it and a release note for the Beaver. "There you go, Jack, she's all yours."

"I'll take your very word for it, Al." Aviation people tend to be a bit on the superstitious side and perhaps so was I, as I made one final attempt. "Say, Al, you wouldn't think you should have given her a little refresher overhaul before lining her up for this flight?"

"Well, we put her through a one-hundred-hour check, which is more than the book requires and we found absolutely nothing that gave any cause for concern." Again he pushed the clipboard in my direction until it somehow inescapably wound up in my hand, repeating the words, "She's all yours, buddy."

"Any squawks?" I had the feeling that he had not told me everything and I was right.

"Well, as a matter of fact, the ELT is u/s. It somehow packed up and I couldn't get a replacement in the shortness of time. But what the hell do you need that for? Just fly properly and you'll be fine."

"Well, if that's all, I can live with it." I was not overly concerned about the ELT, the Emergency Location Transmitter, a gadget that would be activated by the impact of any crash or rough landing to send out a homing signal for potential rescuers. That did not really worry me and I was relieved that there were no compelling reasons to delay my departure. I had already made plans for the weekend and the best of reasons for wanting to get home, first stage being base. I accepted Al's paperwork, countersigned his file copies and went back to the cafeteria hut to get a good meal before our departure.

The flight started unspectacularly enough, like a milk-run should. The engine hummed nicely and all instruments were working properly. One drawback of our Beaver was the rather substandard performance of our cabin heater, for we had to wear full weather gear, including parkas, fur hats, gloves and snow boots in order not to freeze to death during the flight. But as things were to turn out this probably saved our lives.

Without trying very hard I had become the company's favourite special assignments man or bush-pilot, in my own language, the man for non-routine missions like this one. It had been no surprise that I was the first in line to be offered this flight. I could have turned it down; it was my choice. If I had said 'no' it would have been a no without prejudice and it would not be held against me and would not have left a dark spot on my career-sheet. Experience had shown that an unhappy pilot can be a liability. Aviation has some good rules.

I wanted to do the flight.

Yes, definitely, I wanted to get away from where I was, back to base and when I got there away from it! I had my reasons and I wanted to fly the Beaver with its powerful Pratt & Whitney Junior Wasp radial engine, famous not so much on account of the Beaver but rather for powering the DC-3 ever since they started building it prior to World War II in greater numbers than any other aircraft engine.

After about an hour the weather deteriorated rapidly. Maybe more accurately we were catching up with some bad weather, flying into it from behind. As there was no hope of doing this flight under instrument conditions for lack of sufficient navigational aids on the ground I stayed below the clouds, constantly scanning the area ahead and to our left and right for landmarks known to me and quietly plotting them away in my memory banks. I knew all the time where we were, keeping a mental record of this. Meanwhile, Harry had got busy with the flight-following. As was standard Company procedure he called base on the radio every twenty minutes, to give them an update of our position.

As became evident later I was not paying enough attention to Harry's radio messages of flight progress. In fact, let's face it, I was not paying any attention at all to what he was doing. As far as I was concerned, Harry was not relevant to the operation.

He had fixed the navigation chart of our area to a clipboard, which was balancing on his thighs, leaning against the co-pilot's flight control column. About every five minutes he checked compass course, indicated airspeed and altitude. He did some calculations, the nature of which eluded me. Then he jotted down our position on the map as at that time, as he saw it. At the appropriate twenty-minute intervals he would call in the co-ordinates, which were a simple map reference on a horizontal and vertical grid. The

Duty Operations Officer at base would note the positions as they were called in, and that was where you were; the Company's own system, not very scientific but effective, under most circumstances. It was a bit like playing 'Battleships' at school during your math class when the teacher was not looking.

'F48'

'Eh, hmmm . . . destroyer . . . sunk . . .'

'. . . Sorry, buddy.'

The very existence of these grid maps had been Collins' brainchild, of which he was immensely proud, introduced before GPS became readily available. Harry was not at ease with having to figure out our position and call it in. He seemed flustered and fidgeted around with notepad and pocket calculator. At the time I did not notice that, but should have. After all, I was the pilot and therefore responsible.

Both Harry and I were blissfully unaware of the fact that we were flying straight into disaster. It was only afterwards when quietly going through what I remembered that I realised that. Afterwards we always know how to interpret the many little telltale signs that pop up here and there to warn us.

"Yuko."

Her lovely brown eyes reached right into me. She did not look at me, was not holding my gaze, or staring me down. She was looking right into my heart.

"I'm Jack." Our eyes met for a long, timeless moment, during which our hearts and minds fused, became one. The magic of love had swept right over and through us. I had first seen her a week ago, when I had managed to slip in a couple of days of R & R, although, technically speaking, I had gone to Anchorage on official company business. Sushi Hito was my all time favourite restaurant - well, for the time being. I never missed an opportunity to enjoy its delicious food.

I was spellbound, completely knocked off my feet, the very instant I set eyes on her. This was the first occasion that I had found to speak to her except for trivial remarks like 'how are you tonight?' or questions about the menu. I had made inquiries with Noriko.

"New girl, Noriko san?"

"Yes, she came from Tokyo about three weeks ago; musician, violin, used to play in a string quartet, but the cello got married and the other two took up jobs in an orchestra. So she decided to spend some time with Kiyoshi san, our owner. He's her uncle. She's moonlighting as a waitress, waiting for her Green Card to come through, not quite legally." She put a finger to her lips with a conspiratorial expression on her face, swearing me to secrecy as soon as she had told me.

Yuko placed the *Sushi Moriawase* in front of me, her eyes still right inside mine. Under normal circumstances a Japanese woman will lower her eyes after a brief glance at the person facing her. That is considered to be polite behaviour. The Japanese think of the eyes as the gateway into a person's inner self, into which one must not intrude. But this was not intruding. This was Nature taking its course.

"Will you come back?" still looking right into me, leaning forward as if to get inside me.

"Of course, next Saturday; I'll be coming to Anchorage on our mail and supplies flight. We should land round about 11:30 a. m., give or take a little."

"I don't have to work Saturday. I'm free."

"Then let's have lunch together." Our conspiracy was complete.

"Affirmative, base, Beaver out." Harry gave me his usual college boy grin as he put the microphone back into its socket.

"That almost does it for this trip," he added in my direction. "Three more calls and old Collins can go and have his mushroom pizza and get some shuteye."

His words had jerked me back into the present.

Sod him, bloody Harry, I thought. Why the hell did he have to invade my privacy? As I tried to shut Harry out of my mind, my thoughts went back to Yuko who had suddenly appeared at Sushi Hito. Megumi and Noriko had been there ever since I discovered the place on my first visit to Anchorage some two years ago. They were both in their late forties and had been with the establishment since it first opened. Yuko was a little over thirty and still a youngster in my eyes. Each of the other two was very attractive, if not outright beautiful. But for me they were no match for Yuko's graceful charm. Besides, when sparks fly, they fly. What had happened between Yuko and me had been more like a flash of lightning, not just sparks. It had been instantaneous and total. My guarded and polite distance, maintained at the establishment over almost two years, had finally been broken down by the miracle of instant infatuation, being turned head-over-heels, falling in love.

Snap out of it, you stupid bastard! I had to get back on track. You get paid for flying this machine, not for daydreaming. It was time for another instrument check, but all was fine, as of course it should be. The little old Beaver was humming along like clockwork, making me feel completely comfortable and totally relaxed. I was glad I had agreed to do the flight.

The weather continued to deteriorate so that I reduced altitude further, first to three thousand feet above ground, eventually even lower, ducking under the cloud base, lower and lower, until we almost hugged the deck. This was still nothing to worry about. The course that I had selected ran over flat ground. Any mountains were far to the left or right and the stretch ahead was clear of major obstructions all the way to base. This was very much the kind of stuff that we were used to. I was navigating by sight, which is formally referred to as flying VFR or under Visual Flying or Flight Rules, verifying all my navigational measures against factual reference to known or identifiable objects on the ground. Shortly, once we got a bit closer to base, we would be in range to pick up their radio beacon and I could go on instruments from there on, never mind the clouds.

We could raise base on the HF short-wave radio, when we wanted to speak to them, but most navigational transmitters operate in the VHF and UHF frequency range. Their respective radio waves follow straight lines, like the line-of-sight. Therefore, you could only start picking them up once the source that was transmitting popped up above the horizon of your field of vision.

We remained silent, totally relaxed, as the Beaver's engine droned on, each man pursuing his own private thoughts. Then Harry struck up a conversation. Without reference to anything that was going on around us he looked at me sideways, college boy grin, as ever.

"Say, old boy, what's your horizon?"

"My what? I'm afraid you lost me."

"I mean, where do you want to be, say, ten, fifteen years from now, when you get senile or feeble-minded and retire?"

The question baffled me. I had never really thought about that, never tried to develop a strategy for retirement, never given even the slightest thought to the unavoidable geriatric phase of my life that would catch up with me, in due course, unless . . .

"Well, do you want to work until you drop dead, sail around the world, turn religious or what?"

"You know, I really need to think about that."

But before we could take this any further there was a loud bang from ahead of us, followed instantaneously by a bright flash from the direction of the engine. Or maybe it was the other way around, first the flash and then the bang, but whatever it was, it was sudden and absolutely unexpected, without any warning. A large chunk of something blew away. I could not make out what it was. From the corner of my eye I saw what looked like part of the engine cover, viciously hurtling through the air. Whatever it was, it narrowly missed the right half of the windshield and Harry's startled face behind it. The unidentified object slammed into the leading edge of the right wing, ripping deeply into it. Maybe the fuel pump or something even more serious had disintegrated, setting the engine compartment ablaze and starving the engine of fuel.

I only had split seconds to do the pilot's emergency three-hand job . . . . simultaneously feather the engine, cut the throttle, hit the master circuit breaker and fuel main switch and activate the fire extinguisher system in the engine compartment. At the same time I had to continue flying the aircraft, which was decelerating with no more forward propelling power, getting perilously close to stalling speed, below which the aircraft would drop out of the sky like a stone.

We were losing altitude fast as I was pointing the aircraft's nose downward to retain enough forward movement and lift. There was no time for lengthy debates. We were going down. I was searching for some level ground to attempt a landing while the aircraft still had enough speed to fly aerodynamically.

At best this would be a controlled crash.

An inlet was racing up towards us, frozen-over with numerous piles of broken up and refrozen ice and lots of snow-drifts, some of which may have been hiding the odd rock outcrop. Without engine power our speed continued to drop with stalling imminent. I searched for a sufficiently large stretch of unobstructed ground, to set down the aircraft and jump free, given the fire on board. We could feel its heat through the instrument panel, with flames licking up the outside of the windshield. The fire extinguisher system in the engine compartment had not succeeded completely in putting out the fire. It had just slowed it down, buying us some more, vitally needed seconds to land. Ahead of us, slightly to our right, I saw a gap between two mounds of snow and pointed the aircraft's nose towards it. With ground contact imminent I pulled back on the stick to get the nose up on impact and avoid going head-over-heels.

On first contact a flash of white, powdery snow instantaneously engulfed everything with explosive ferocity, blasting into the cockpit, momentarily blinding and choking us. I could not see a thing. The first few yards on the ground felt like the snow was soft and deep. We were sliding over the ground just as with water skiing, when you have let go of the rope and wait to sink in. With deceleration and the loss of aerodynamic lift the aircraft's weight shifted from being carried by the wing to the undercarriage, which was now digging in. We slowed down. Then the left wheel hit a solid object, hidden in the deep, soft snow, maybe stacks of ice or a rock outcrop. As the wheel strut collapsed the aircraft was jerked sharply to the left, hobbling along in a bumpy, circular movement, until the right wheel struck another solid object and also collapsed, to knock us back on a straight course. The wings were now closer to the ground, hitting things and disintegrating in successive stages. Then, abruptly, the nose dug in sharply, stopping the aircraft on the spot, bringing up the fuselage momentarily in a forward tilting movement, lingering for an instant as if held up by some invisible force and then, with a subdued thud, dropping back into the deep snow.

Burying the aircraft's nose in the snowdrift for the moment stemmed the flames in the engine compartment, long enough to give us time to undo the safety harnesses. They had stopped us from going through the windshield but could not prevent me from hitting my head on something, which felt like a blow with a sledge-hammer.

It took me a few seconds to catch my breath, figure out which way was up or down, fumble for the door and get out. The fire had not stopped completely. It had rekindled itself and found its way to the aircraft's fuel tanks; maybe there had been sparks when the aircraft tore apart.

Most modern aircraft have their fuel tanks built into the wing, which puts them at a comfortable distance from the cockpit, but not so the Beaver. Its main tank was in the belly. That meant that you were sitting on the fuel tank, all the more reason to get away from the aircraft as fast as possible. I yelled a warning shout in the general direction of Harry. From the corner of my eye I could see him getting out on the other side.

We had not covered more than a few paces when tanks were exploding and the whole aircraft went up in fire and smoke, preventing us from going back to grab a few essential things and then making a dash for it. Miraculously I was holding the Flight-Safety-Kit in my hand, an emergency box, located next to the pilot's left foot position, which I must have instinctively picked up on my way out.

Once outside we stumbled away from the burning wreck, both of us reaching a little mound out of harm's way and slumping down in the snow, wondering what went wrong and what to do next. Then I noticed that I was experiencing a fierce pain in my head from the blow and in the shoulders, where the safety harness had dug itself into my body.

For what seemed like an eternity we were unable to say a word, trying to catch our breath and recover mentally. Slowly we tried to take stock and accept our predicament. All things considered it could have been worse. We looked at each other to make sure the other was OK. We were both still alive and in one piece. That was the good news. The bad news was only a few moments away. As we sat there the shock of aircraft loss and crash set in, making the adrenaline pump violently. It took long moments for us to calm down sufficiently to start looking at the situation. No matter how tough or brave you are, the first reaction is one of dismay, shock, horror and naked fear, in no particular order but in spades. Slowly, very slowly, we managed to function again, start discussing the situation and what our options were.

"You know, Harry, things could be a lot worse." I thought a little morale-boosting wouldn't be a mistake. "We have these safety and survival briefings from time to time. On the last occasion they told us all about a number of little cottages, now deserted and empty, that had been built in the fur-trapper era. The people from *Fish and Wildlife* had identified some of the better ones and provided them with basic emergency rations. One of them should be close by. We must have flown right over it less than a minute ago. Let's try and find it."

"Yeah, sounds like a brilliant idea." A faint smile of relief brightened up Harry's face.

"For all we know this might turn into an unexpected vacation." I didn't really think we had any reason to celebrate but I wanted to make sure that we were throwing some positive energy at the problem.

Then it came, the totally unexpected shock on top of everything else. Seeking some reassurance I tried to verify with Harry our last position that he had radioed through to Base.

"We're at M06/206 N06/207," I said to Harry. "Thank God they know that at Base."

"No . . ." Harry hesitated, obviously afraid to come out with some really bad news, ". . . they don't." He turned to me with that frightened-rabbit-look in his eyes, hesitated some more, fidgeted around with something that he was holding in his hands and finally spoke as if with an oversized lump in his throat. "That isn't what I said in my last call to base. I had - us at - N06/201 M06/202."

"You had what?" I stared at him in disbelief.

"Well, that's where I thought we were." He sounded like a kid that has been caught with his hand in the cookie jar. "You must have heard it when I spoke to Collins."

Well, I should have but I had not. Used to flying alone, I had lost the habit of checking on what the other person in the cockpit was doing, when there was one, an oversight that could cost us dearly, fatally, if things went as bad as for an instant I thought they might.

He had been with the company and in Alaska for almost a year, but so far Harry's flying had been mostly very short supply flights between the landing strip or helipad of the field station to which he was attached at the time and one or other of the many oil rigs and pumping installations that were usually grouped within, at the most, twenty minutes' flying. The field stations had radio homing beacons to help you find your way back, if the weather suddenly turned bad while you were away. But other than that, his flying had always been visual. He was probably not yet used to magnetic aberrations near the pole and may have been insufficiently aware of the effect of a ten-knot crosswind that can shift you sideways quite a bit, given the length of a flight.

So Harry had worked out a position that after about two hours of flight put us almost twenty miles further to the west, right in the middle of Gollong-Gollong, where we would now be quite dead, scattered across the side of a steep mountain, had we actually been there and forced to land. Harry had radioed it through to base about two minutes before disaster struck. It would be at least another eighteen, plus a little extra, before Collins would start missing us and raise the alarm.

It would have been really nice if we had been able to get a distress call off when things started going wrong. But I had been too busy with all the other urgent things that I had to do, including flying the aircraft and trying to land before we fell out of the sky, whilst Harry was visibly overpowered by the vicious turn of events. I could not blame him for that. This was just a case of tough luck. I am not sure whether I in his place would have acted differently. It takes a certain experience on top of presence of mind. Besides, let us not forget that he was just a passenger, if you want to look at things formally. I should have shouted an order for him.

"Harry, call base!"

The time between the explosion and hitting the ground was less than half a minute, maybe as little as twenty seconds. You cannot expect miracles. It was a miracle that we got out of the aircraft not merely alive, bruised and battered, but on the whole in good enough shape. Distress call or not we had to start facing facts. Whatever was responsible for the wrong location data that somehow reached base was history. It had nothing to do with the fuel pump or whatever caused the explosion and the forced landing, but it bode ill for our hopes of a quick rescue and – perhaps – even survival. It meant that the chance that someone might actually come looking for us at our present location was remote . . . . nil?

"We've got to figure out what to do next," I said to Harry as we both struggled back on our feet.

"This thing got an ELT?" asked Harry, his voice holding the hope that we actually did have an Emergency Location Transmitter on board.

"Well, it does and it doesn't work. There was something wrong with it and they were going to put a new one in once we got back to base."

"Fat lot of good that does us," remarked Harry, more to himself, for I had turned away to inspect the wreck more closely.

Famous last words, I thought, remembering when Al Hickman had told me earlier that morning that the Beaver's ELT was u/s, as he had put it, unserviceable, not working. The ELT was not mandatory and not on the MEL, the Minimum Equipment List for a relatively short and straightforward non-revenue ferry flight. It looked like we were adding fast to our negative options.

It was obvious that the burnt-out wreck offered no support of any kind and would soon be turned into just another snowdrift, indistinguishable from thousands of others. To anybody looking for us from the air it most certainly would not provide any visual guidance. Of that I was absolutely certain. I had been on too many airborne search and rescue missions in the Arctic, more than one of them, sadly, unsuccessful.

"Staying at the wreck without ELT would be a bloody waste of time." More to myself - not at all sure whether Harry would listen,

"No! Hell no, I disagree! Let's dig in at the wreck and wait for help. They're bound to come looking for us here, sooner or later." It was hope rather than secure knowledge that made Harry say that as well as the desire to avoid a decision of which he did not know the consequences. Nor did I of course, but we had to make it.

"Let's stop kidding ourselves, Harry." I was not going to freeze to death, hanging out on hope. "What do you suppose you would see from, say, as low as a thousand feet above ground? Say you're not flying directly overhead but about five, six hundred yards sideways. What significant marks would stand out, with us, frozen stiff and solid, huddled against whatever is left of the wreck, snow piling on top of it fast and us by its side? Like I said, there are a couple of old fur-trappers' shacks on the shore, at least on the map, one of them only about half a mile from here, due south-east and right underneath our flight-path. If we keep going back in the direction we came we should be able to find it and get some shelter from the cold before we freeze to death. I want to go home, even if it takes a little longer than planned, not die here, don't you?"

"Sure as hell I want to go home, too." Harry was resigning himself to the inevitable. His voice carried little or no conviction. Judging by the sound of it, we were already as good as dead. We left it at that and looked around for anything to take along with us.

"Well, let's get cracking. It will be dark soon. If we don't find the shack on the shore straight away let's look for a place where we can shelter for the night and look for it in the morning, once it gets light. The longer we screw around, the less time we'll have to get sorted out. This is a toss-up between certain death, staying here and all the hope in the world by taking things into our own hands. Even if they come and find us, when do you reckon that will be? Not tonight, for sure, and if the weather stays this bad or gets even worse, it could be days. Let's be realistic and get off this open, unprotected ground to somewhere where we can hole up. If we stay here that ice-cold wind will kill us within hours."

With that sobering prospect before us we started trekking off in a direction where I thought we might encounter some life forms other than the swarms of fish, separated from us by the thick ice, that is if there were any. We headed straight for the shoreline of the inlet that we could just make out in the evening haze and the blur from the cold.

I'm gonna miss my luncheon date with Yuko!

When that thought flashed through my mind reality had finally caught up with me. I had crash-landed an aircraft in the arctic wilderness and for all intents and purposes my mission was over. So much for flying home. What next? My inner voice came on loud and clear: Survive! You stupid sonofabitch! Survive, survive! That's an order. Isn't that what they trained you to do way back when you were a young lad in the RAF? Besides, you've got goals, things you want to do, haven't you?

"Come on, Harry, let's go. Get your ass in gear and let's get cracking." I wasn't really being fair to him, but I had to let out my anger and Harry was the only one there on whom I could let it out. It's a mean bad world. After all, I had been the one flying the now crashed aircraft, not him.

I picked up the Flight-Safety-Kit and a piece of loose panelling that had managed to stay in good shape. It had been thrown clear of the aircraft before everything burst into flames. Harry grabbed some other bits and pieces that would come in handy later for creating shelter. So, we set out to the south-east, laboriously making our way through the deep snow, sinking in at every step we took, sometimes going down headlong. I felt suddenly very tired, whilst over the last few moments Harry had gathered some fresh energy.

Then I heard a thudding noise. The rescue helicopter, I thought, but it was only the blood pounding in my head. My knees got wobbly and I fell into the snow a couple of times. The icy wind hit my face. With all the excitement I had not noticed it quite that much but now it was bordering on the unbearable.

It was getting dark fast, hard to see what was up ahead, just that there was a shoreline rising out of the ice and snow no more than a couple of hundred yards away. Then I heard Harry shout my name from about half a mile away and when I looked to my right he was there next to me, catching me in his arms just as I was about to fall again. More stumbling than walking I went on, following in Harry's tracks. It got even darker, sky and snow blurred and became indistinguishable, shapes and contours absorbed by a featureless eternity of arctic nothingness.

Suddenly a bright light erupted in the centre of my field of vision, as if someone had set off a photoflash right in my face, blinding me temporarily. As the effect wore off and my vision slowly returned I was looking directly into two beautiful dark-brown eyes, more black than dark brown. They were looking back at me out of a face that I could not distinguish clearly from its surroundings. I did not recognise it. The face strangely merged with the background so that only the image of the eyes remained clearly visible for a few more moments, until the darkness absorbed them again along with the rest of the image.

Xola

The name flashed through my mind. The eyes had a name! They belonged to Xola! Dark-brown, black eyes looking at me out of a face that had emerged briefly out of the dark, only to cruelly retreat back into it before I could recognise it. Who had said the name? I had clearly and distinctly heard it.

"You all right, Jack?" Harry was bending over me as I lay headlong face down in the deep, cold snow.

"Yeah . . . I'm OK . . . just a little dizzy." I was slowly struggling back onto my feet, grateful to accept Harry's helping arm. "Come to think of it, I must have received a pretty serious bang on the head when we went over and didn't notice it quite that much with all the excitement. Now it's coming through. A double scotch would certainly be a big boost!" We both had to laugh.

"Who were you talking to? You said something just now." Despite the fading light I could make out a puzzled look on Harry's face.

"Never said a word - not that I can think of – at any rate," turning away from him to resume my struggle against the deep snow, this time moving ahead of him, making for the shoreline, barely visible as just a darker shade of dark. All of a sudden they were there; I mean I saw them! They may have been there all along, just ahead of us and to our left and right, shadows, moving shadows: We were surrounded by a group of shadows. Then I could make them out very clearly, despite the increasing darkness: Wolves, about a dozen of them, one of them no more than six feet away from me, facing me, not moving, looking me right in the eye.

Xola! Again that name flashed through my mind.

Xola, the wolf with a name. At that moment I did not care why this wolf obviously had a name nor that it had communicated with me. I was frightened, excited and at the same time very tired, exhausted, all energy drained from my body. Then it struck me that despite all else at that moment I had just one desire: To cuddle up in the arms of a beautiful, loving woman. I was longing for my woman, my very own woman. I was longing for love, the love of my woman. I was looking at beautiful dark-brown, black eyes, the most fabulous eyes, the eyes of my woman.

"You'd better move on!" Harry almost bumped into me from behind as I had slowed down again and then stopped completely. "We're almost there, the shore, I mean. Let's look for shelter there."

For a brief moment Harry and I stood there in silence, looking at dark, featureless silhouettes, barely visible, blurred by haze, drifting snow and darkness. Neither he nor I said a word. It seemed like an endless silence.

From this point onwards my recollections get a bit thin. I remember that wolves were milling around us and coaxing us on in a distinct direction. Suddenly we came up short on the embankment, which rose steeply out of the ground. We struggled upwards. As we reached the top it stood there right in front of us, out of nowhere and at this moment totally unexpected: the cabin!

"Harry, you reckon the wolves showed us the way to this place?"

"What wolves? What are you talking about? I saw no wolves - we just got lucky."

Once safely inside the cabin neither of us talked. We just wanted to curl up in a corner. The dramatic experience of aircraft loss and the fear of dying in a ball of fierce flames were demanding their right. Lighting a fire in the little stove from the kindling and bits and pieces that we found was Boy Scouts' instinct. All we could do was to grab the blankets, which – miracle - had been left in the cabin. As we were to discover later, at daybreak, the cabin had actually been quite well prepared by some kind soul to serve as an emergency shelter for some poor suckers just like us, as and when the occasion arose, if ever.

I drifted off into a diffuse nirvana, the never-never land where things were right and all was fine, the very instant that I crawled under my blanket. I must have gone straight into a deep sleep of exhaustion, like falling into a bottomless black hole.

Then I was in a confined compartment, being turned head over heels in the dark, with flashes passing before my eyes of wolves rushing towards me head on, continuing right through me as they reached me. Then I was sitting inside the cockpit of the Beaver. As I looked out of the little side window I saw a wolf, flying alongside the aircraft. It did not have wings but was floating through the air like Superman and his friends, defying all notions of known types and methods of flight, be they ballistic, lighter-than-air or aerodynamic. This was obviously the fourth method: Levitation. The flying wolf wore sunglasses, smoked a cigarette, smiled at me and looked like Susan Henry from the Company's typing pool, better known as 'the Company's cover girl' for having appeared on the cover of *The Alaska Fisherman*, last July.

For Chrissake, I thought. I'm dead.

I looked to my right and saw Harry, also smiling at me. He had a wolf's head and wore a smart Royal Air Force flight jacket, complete with white scarf and all. On the upper right of his uniform there was a nameplate, which read 'Parker' and on the left were his wings and an impressive band of medals and distinctions. His rank was that of Squadron Leader.

Wow! My word, I thought. What does that make me? I looked down at myself, searching for clues. Air Vice-Marshall was the least that I should have expected.

Jesus!

My furry hands were casually playing on the controls. That was all the proof I needed. I was dead. No doubt about it. Could have been worse, I thought after a while as I did not feel any pain or other discomfort. The warmth of a body was pressing against my side. As I was about to put my fist squarely between Harry's eyes I managed to check that movement just in time, before I would have hit Yuko. I looked into her lovely eyes as she cuddled her sleek furry body against mine. She had the loveliest wolf body I had ever seen. Something was stirring on my left. As I turned I saw the wolf snuggling up to me that I recognised as the one that had introduced herself as Xola. I looked back at Yuko, then realised that I was a wolf tucked in cosily between two female wolves. We all had wolves' bodies and wolves' heads with human facial features, including Xola, who looked as lovely as Yuko, alas different, clearly different with a beautiful face and those wonderful dark-brown-black eyes! They both put their paws around my neck and I could feel wolves' tongues caressing my ears. It was the most delightful feeling that I could imagine. I had arrived in wolves' heaven. This was final proof. I was definitely dead.

Then I heard the howling of the wind outside, rattling something, maybe a shutter or part of the roof. So I was not dead after all. In a state of half sleep I was thinking about what had happened, about the wolves, those wonderful, fabulous wolves that - miracle of miracles - had led us to the cabin; I could swear they had, who else if not they? In due course we would have found it by ourselves, maybe the next morning, as we had a good enough general idea of where to go looking for it, but first we would have had to survive a night out in the unprotected wilds of Alaska.

In a state of half-sleep my thoughts kept going back to the wolves. I had seen wolves at close range before, remembering the coyotes in Arizona, where I spent some time as a kid and the wolves of East Africa, where I was born. But these wolves were special, the Xola wolf and her pack, whose name I knew.

How - why?

She must have said it, how else could I know it?

I was wide-awake now, unable to go back to sleep. Bizarre images appeared again and again as if part of the reality with Xola levitating through the air, circling around me with outstretched arms - front legs.

Suddenly I was overcome by a deep sense of shame. I had failed in the principal objective of my mission. A severe case of deeply hurt aviator's pride gripped hold of me. If at all I would return to base without my aircraft, mission incomplete!

Shit! We don't do that, do we?

We are professionals, getting things done, properly and with style and class, always at the leading edge of our trade. I was lying on a bunk bed in a dark cabin somewhere in northern Alaska, minus aircraft, minus pride, minus a good measure of self-respect.

Failure! Shit! Shit! Shit!

I was no longer going home!

Then, seemingly without any connection to the events of the day, the thought hit me like a thunderbolt. Here I was, an aviator pushing past his prime, who had not only failed in his mission but in his whole life. No woman had ever said to me the three magic words:

I love you.

Never ever. Not once. Not a single one of the bloody lot of them. Not ever. Surely, not one of them had said these words to me, even if once only.

If my life were to end now it would have been a life without love. With that thought a deep sadness came over me – a sense of total loss – a complete failure in life.

After a lot of tossing and turning deep and uninterrupted sleep finally came, with no more levitating wolves, aircraft going ballistic and co-pilots with wolves' heads.

Meanwhile . . .

The who is Jack and Harry; the rest is dunno.
Bad news breaks.

"Attention, emergency response team . . . we'll meet in operations ASAP. We have a missing Beaver, two souls." Collins' voice droned over the intercom.

Bob Masters, the chief engineer, was the first to join Bill Collins, the company's director of flight operations, who was also the shift duty officer and hence already there. He was quickly followed by Hank Snyder, a helicopter pilot, Paul Baxter from logistics planning, Teresa Sullivan, the medic, Roger Prescott, the manager and Scott Raleigh, pilot and licensed mechanic.

"What's up?" Hank Snyder was the first to ask the obvious question.

"Beaver's gone missing." Collins sat down at the large, all-purpose table, which on happier occasions had supported such functions as the Fourth-of-July do and the company Christmas party. Collins had spread out a copy of the grid map. On it apart from the grid and the topographical features were a number of lines, one of which had been highlighted with a yellow marker pen. This one obviously represented the course of the Beaver as it had been called in to base, a succession of crosses that had been connected by a pencil line. It started at Camp Bravo, the point of origin, ran due south for fifty miles, then turned right about fifteen degrees. It continued from there in a straight line until it ended in the middle of nowhere, roughly thirty miles before it would have collided with a mountain range, rising to the respectable height of over eight thousand feet that was lying right in its path. The crosses, marking the position as reported every twenty minutes, were almost exactly fifty miles apart, which tallied with the Beaver's cruising speed of about 150 miles per hour. Everybody looked at the map, trying to take in important details so as not to waste time asking redundant questions.

"OK, I'll ask the obvious: Who, what, and why?" Paul Baxter had managed to wrap everybody's questions into one.

Collins took his time. Then, tapping the rubber-tipped eraser end of his five-cent pencil on the grid map, he said, "The who is Jack and Harry and the rest is dunno." He paused, taking another long look at the map. "Jack and Harry were ferrying the old Beaver back here . . ."

"I didn't know we still had a Beaver." Hank Snyder was obviously not yet aware of the fact that someone had declared an emergency.

"Shut up, asshole," hissed Scott Raleigh. Apart from having a general dislike for helicopter pilots, being a fixed-wing man himself, there had been bad chemistry between him and Hank Snyder ever since he first set eyes on him.

"Thank you." Collins, who shared Raleigh's dislike for the brash chopper pilot, hinted a nod of the head in his direction. "I couldn't have responded more appropriately. Now, if I may continue. Jack left Camp Bravo at 1:20 p. m., local time, in command of our Beaver N66KP, ETA Base 4:25 p. m. Harry Parker was in the right seat as a passenger, more or less. They made the statutory position progress reports, as you can see on this map. They were all made right on the button, at the top of the hour, twenty past and twenty to. The last one came in at 3:20 p. m. sharp; after that – nothing, no call at 3:40, none at 4:00, none at 4:20, no distress call, no attempt to raise us. They just went silent. It's now 5:05 and still nothing. At about 4:55 their fuel would have run out. So, we have to deduce that they are down. It's practically dark now, so there's nothing we can do for now except keep a radio watch."

"I can take a trip over there in the Huey." Hank Snyder was trying to make good some lost terrain.

"It's a brave offer, Hank, but I have to say no on the grounds of the local weather situation. You wouldn't be able to see a thing, even if you flew right overhead their position. Besides . . . sorry, I don't want to lose another ship." Collins was all mission control. "You all mark the last known position plus whatever they would have covered in the nineteen minutes thereafter and up to the next call-in. Since all their earlier calls were bang on time we have to assume that whatever happened did so between their last call and the next nineteen . . . twenty minutes. OPS remain open and manned all night. We'll gather here at 7:00 a. m. tomorrow morning. Subject to weather we'll launch a two-ship search party at first light. Scott, you fly the Twin Otter and take along Bob as additional observer. An extra pair of eyes won't be a mistake in that white wilderness. Hank, you gas up the Huey to the hilt and follow half an hour after the Otter to a position that they will give you over the air, once they see something."

"And if they see nothing?"

"You launch anyway, to be near the scene . . . just in case." He had made a long pause and everybody in the room knew what that meant: to pick up and bring back the boys in body bags, assuming that *seeing nothing* actually meant seeing the one thing you did not want to see.

"Teresa, you go with Hank. Draw a full emergency medical kit. You never know." Collins took another long look at the map. "Any questions?" His eyes went slowly from one to the other as if to impress on everybody the seriousness of the situation. He took his time, doing another end-to-end scan of the grid map, before he added, "well," another pause and a sigh. This affected him more than one would have expected. Then he snapped back into mission control mode. "Let's get the gear ready for tomorrow. We can talk about it some more over dinner. Meeting's adjourned."

The Cabin

Day 2
"My life's gonna be over and nobody will ever know I was there. There won't even be a grave for somebody to put flowers on. Nobody will come on my birthday."
Harry's outcry . . .

When I woke up in an unfamiliar, dark cottage, lying on a bunk bed, covered with a crude blanket and all my clothes on, the first thing I remembered was a sleep of exhaustion that had taken me into Wolfland with airborne wolves and all the rest. The next thought that occurred to me was the things I remembered from last night and the grave, sobering consequences: my trip home had been cruelly terminated. Over, finished, no more going home.

Slowly we were settling into our new reality of life, accepting our situation and trying to manage as best we could. Finding the cabin, albeit with the help of the wolves – I was now even more convinced - had been a wonderful development, not at all unexpected on my part, as I had known that there was a string of abandoned fur trappers' cottages along the shore. Some of them were actually marked on the map. About a year ago during the fall a field team from the Fish and Wildlife Department had gone around taking stock of the situation and mapping the better ones. I remembered reading in a wildlife magazine that some of the cottages had been stocked with basic survival supplies, just in case, for whomever.

During the first few hours after daybreak and my apparent black-out Harry and I tried to assimilate what had happened. The help from the wolves was not uncontroversial between us. I wanted to talk to him about it now that we were in relative comfort and safety. I was not in very good shape when the alleged event had happened. Harry even said that *I had lost it a bit.* I remembered being surrounded by a wolf pack at close quarters and nudged and pushed on up the embankment so that we arrived in front of the cabin door, right smack in the middle.

"Harry, at least you have to admit that you saw the wolves!"

"What wolves? I saw no wolves. It was pitch-dark, windy, snow was blowing in every direction and visibility was next to nil. I definitely saw no wolves."

"But they were un-miss-able! They were all over us, around us, milling around, left, right and centre and they made sure we found the cabin."

"Luck, we somehow stumbled across it."

"But all the commotion, surely you must have noticed something. What did you see?"

"Well . . . I saw some shapes; doglike shapes."

"Wolves!"

"Dogs!"

"Wolves! For crying out loud, Harry, use your senses! Dogs in the middle of the arctic wilderness, just like that? Why, where are they now and why didn't they stick around for a pat on the head? Dogs would do that."

"So you reckon we saw wolves?"

"Definitely, at least a dozen. And their lead animal licked my ears. Her name is Xola."

"Holy mother of Jesus! For Chrissake, Jack, don't you *ever* mention anything like that to anyone. The Flight Surgeon will have you grounded for the rest of your life for mental instability. I'm sure this Shola spoke to you!"

"Xola, her name is Xola and she did say it to me, how else should I know?"

"Jack, I think you still have a fever. Take a good rest. Maybe there is some Aspirin in the Flight-Safety Kit. I'll see if I can find something here to fix us some tea."

"Don't mother me, Harry, I'm fine. Let's try and take stock of this place. It may be our home for some days to come."

"For our last and final days if nobody comes to get us out of here." Harry had used up a lot of energy putting me straight. Now he was crawling back into his shell again. But this suited me well. I didn't feel like having a long debate. Neither of us did, we were just too tired.

"So, we saw no good-Samaritan wolves, understood?" Harry looked straight at me with a serious face like I never saw him before, without his usual smile. "No wolves! I want to keep my pilot's license. This is America, Jack, not merry old England. Go to Disneyland if you want talking animals. In aviation you've got to deal with serious people like the FAA. That excludes any sense of humour per se or else . . ."

"What's the else?"

"They send you to the funny farm."

At that point I realised that I would have a problem on my hands if I insisted on the wolf aspect. I decided to keep my mouth shut about it in the future. After all, who knows, maybe I did have a fever, was hallucinating. Perhaps Harry was right.

Except: . . . why did I have that name on my mind, almost constantly . . ? Xola. And this Xola wolf looked me in the eye. I could swear to that, FAA or no FAA. And then there was another thought that took a hold of me: Why Xola? Why was there a wolf with a name? Or was that perhaps somebody else's name . . . if so, whose? And why wasn't Yuko the first name that came to my mind? That was certainly strange. And there were those unforgettable beautiful eyes!

Our cottage was a crude little log cabin, measuring about twenty by twenty feet square, sitting on an east-west alignment. There was a door facing south and a tiny window in the middle of each of the other three walls and the door. Inside there were two double-decker bunk berths with a few vintage-looking blankets to accommodate up to four people, a small cast-iron stove, a crude makeshift table and three three-legged stools, plus one with only two legs, lying on its side.

Fixed to the wall next to the door there were a very basic first aid box on one side and a small provisions and tools wall chest on the other. The beds stood along the north side of the room, their ends about six feet apart with the window in the middle. The space between the beds had been used by some kind soul to store firewood up to the windowsill. There was more firewood on the south side, between the stove and the door. And there was even more firewood outside, barely visible under the snow, as I noticed when I stuck my head briefly out the door.

That was good. If we managed our resources carefully that promised a bit of warmth for the next five days to a week or thereabouts, maybe longer if we were economical with it. The first aid kit was vintage stuff, as first aid kits come; primarily bandages, iodine, a pair of scissors and to my utter amazement a Swiss army knife, the officer's version with a can opener and a number of other gadgets. Then there were a few sealed watertight plastic packages, which I would investigate later, except one containing a supply of matches, which I had found and opened first thing on arrival. So the prospect was much better than one would have expected.

A hell of a lot better than we deserved to find!

The provisions and tools wall chest contained about two dozen cans that looked like what I remembered from my RAF days long ago, resembling military surplus supplies or standard rations, cans with no labels but stencilled-on letters like b-e-e-f or p-o-r-k and numbers, which could have been dates, all that painted onto the metal in black. Quite probably they were processed beef and pork of some kind, all probably frozen solid. Then there were a couple of boxes of crackers and to my amazement a handful of packages of dried dates and figs. Whoever had put this together deserved a lot of praise, for this meant survival for at least a week to ten days, unless we got depressed and killed each other before we ran out of food.

But the most unexpected item was the little fixed-frequency crystal transmitter, which at first I almost overlooked, hidden behind the corned beef. Let me quickly lower your expectations before hopes get too high. It was no more than about a handful of wire, a coil, a condenser and what looked like the crystal, about sixty-five cents-worth of hardware in all, like a DIY-set for ten-year old radio enthusiasts. How the hell it got here didn't really matter, it opened up a perspective, no matter how narrow.

This news was loads better than what I would have expected under any circumstances. The only other thing that could have made my joy even more complete would have been a bottle of scotch, stashed away somewhere. But let us not become greedy or ungrateful! We were looking at a distinct survival scenario, nothing more challenging than an adventure trip with the Boy Scouts in my school days.

This was going to be child's play!

When the first flurry of excitement about our discoveries was over we settled into what was to become our principal activity for the next few days, slumped into a corner on the bunk and doing nothing. We had got the fire going again, opened two of the cans and had a real feast on some corned beef and pork stew, confirming my assumption that we were looking at ex-military rations, most likely from surplus stocks - which tasted great.

By late morning we had recovered to about eighty out of a hundred on my scale – as far as I was concerned. I had a splitting headache and pains in my shoulders and arms but nothing really serious to worry about. We had nothing on our agenda for the time being other than waiting for rescue and thinking about what we could do to speed it along. Time would fix the headache and the pains. This was our first chance to relax since the rough landing. Things were now beginning to look distinctly positive. But whilst my mood improved measurably from one moment to the next, Harry's went in the opposite direction. In the first critical phase he had held up much better than I, which must have used up much of his nervous energy. With the relaxation he lost a good part of his assertiveness.

"Jack, I'm gonna die."

"Bullshit." I tried to cheer him up. "You look as fit and healthy as I've ever seen you. What's wrong?"

"I can't read. See that can? I know it's corned beef, but I can't figure out the writing. It just blurs in front of my eyes. I tried to write, just now and I couldn't do it. I'm going blind, Jack!"

"Rubbish, Harry. There's nothing serious affecting you. Maybe you're snow blind. The wind, the blinding-white glare from the snow, maybe the flash from the explosion, the excitement and the exhaustion – it's only normal that you should show some kind of reaction."

"It's a whole lot worse than that. I can feel I'm going blind."

"That's only temporary, I'm sure." Now I had to work on him. "Maybe a mild case of post-crash syndrome, it won't last - it'll be OK by tomorrow, I'm sure. Besides, on the can there are just a few letters and numbers, nothing much to read. And it's pretty dark in here."

"No, it's nothing like that. I'm not snow-blind and it ain't whatever syndromes. It's those damned dogs – wolves. They're spooky, Jack. This is not normal. Maybe your Shola dog put a curse on me."

"Xola," I cut in. "Xola wolf. So you did see her? First you said you saw nothing and now it's *spooky*?"

"Shola, Xola, dog, wolf, same deal. The damned animals put a curse on me. All this is not real."

Then I realised that same as I Harry must have suffered some effect that was now taking its toll, maybe not just a knock on the head but having been thrown around from side to side, when we half-somersaulted with the aircraft. It would seem a miracle if we had got out of all that totally unaffected, even if we had not banged our heads or not noticed having done so in all the turmoil. Stopping an aircraft dead in its tracks even at - say - fifty miles per hour and flipping it over could still expose you to something like four times the force of gravity, four g-s or four times your own weight. We both could have suffered a concussion, the effects of which would be felt only gradually, over some time.

Harry now just didn't want to shut up but went to some length to explain that he thought that there was witchcraft involved. He thought it was quite possible that the *dogs* were trying to kill him. I thought it funny that he could not readily bring himself to say the word *wolf*. It was still *dog* first. Could it just be that he was remembering more than he was prepared to admit? I wonder what he really saw – and for that matter I myself. Something here was *unusual* - to put it mildly.

"Harry, maybe there was something that you saw that put the living daylights into you, in a manner of speaking. Maybe you're just not consciously aware of it. Something you saw that shocked you, terrified you. And as for your eyesight being affected, I think that could be explained as pretty normal, all things considered. I know from examples in the past that that won't last. Your 20/20 vision will be back in no time, just give your eyes a rest."

"And if it doesn't?" I was amazed at the sudden change that had taken hold of him. The energy with which he had confronted me earlier and put me straight had gone completely. He looked like a man who had stared death directly in the eye. He was ashen and I thought I could actually see him tremble a little.

"I'm definitely under a spell. It's wicked; feels like my head is in a vies. I'm scared, Jack, really scared, I think I'm gonna die."

There was a long pause. Then he added in a very low voice, which, as he continued, almost turned into a whisper. "My life's gonna be over and nobody will ever know I was there. There won't even be a grave for somebody to put flowers on. Nobody will come on my birthday . . ."

"For crying out loud, Harry, We're gonna be just fine. We'll sit it out for a few days until base gets organised and they come and get us. As far as I'm concerned this is a paid vacation."

"Don't try to humour me, Jack. I know it's serious. I am really scared that I'm gonna die, Jack . . ." He let his voice trail off.

I saw him shake but that could have been the cold. He looked even paler now than before and altogether not well. Bloody panic! I thought. That's the last thing we need now. You survive in the head and this guy is giving himself up for dead. Then I realised that Harry was suffering a fever that seemed to have gained momentum as he relaxed his conscious efforts and slumped into passivity. The fever would explain his change of attitude - and it would blow over.

I remembered an occasion many years ago in Tanzania when we were in a convoy of three Land Rovers. One drove over the side of a low bridge and fell some twenty feet into a shallow river. None of the three people in the vehicle got killed and they all seemed OK at first but as time went on one of them increasingly went into a state of *I'm-gonna-die-syndrome*, just like Harry now. So something like this probably has to be taken seriously. At the time the man affected went from normal right after the accident to almost dying in a matter of half a day but he got back on track. Harry would surely snap out of it too.

I wanted to keep my newly regained optimism and therefore refused to worry. He would be fine. And my general discomfort got less and less by the hour, much as Harry's seemed to drive towards a climax.

"Harry, snap out of it! You're gonna live."

But all my encouragement had the opposite effect on him and only hardened his resolve to die. He was deliberately dying, as if just plain dying wasn't enough for him. Then he plucked up his courage and opened up towards me, to tell me what he really wanted. With his impending death looming large before his eyes he wanted to record for posterity the essence of what he had come to understand about the one great central issue of his life. I am saying this as pompously as Harry put it to me.

"Jack, when we came down and there was the fire, I had things flashing through my mind, like a two-hour movie in one second."

"Yeah, that makes sense, I can relate to that. I've had a few of them myself over the years."

"I saw that my life is being messed up, restrained as if I'm in chains, caught up in something that weighs me down. I need to get that off my chest; tell somebody about it, work it out. You're the only one here. Please, listen to me. Write it down for me. It's important. I think my life's all screwed up." After a short pause he added: "I'm so depressed. Let me tell you about something in my past that keeps coming back to me and affects my daily life – not just like memories would – it takes hold of my daily life, controls it. Help me work things out."

"What is it?"

"It's about a woman that has taken possession of me and is running my life."

"Wow, Harry, that makes sense! Now we're talking! Why didn't you say so in the first place? That must be serious," I said, half jokingly – but Harry remained – dead – and I mean *absolutely* dead serious.

At first I wanted to refuse. A man never likes to get into another man's personal sphere. But he insisted so vehemently that I finally caved in and promised to write it all down as best I could remember, once we got back home. On that he exploded!

"No, no, you've got to write it down now, in case we both die! Promise me that!"

Under normal circumstances I would have been outraged at his lack of confidence. But I could not take any more of this without going around the bend myself. So I agreed to his *dying wish* and promised to write it down as soon as possible. That soothed his anxiety for the moment.

I stoked up our little cabin fire. We settled down and Harry started delivering what much to my surprise and against all expectations turned out to be a most extraordinary story. I still had some misgivings. I could relate to aviation matters and this was going to be extremely personal.

There was the hope that I could still get out of this unique experience if Collins and his mob showed up in time and pulled us out of the shit. However, for right now that did not seem very likely. It was snowing heavily, visibility was down to zero and the chance of conducting an aerial search with even the remotest hope of success was nil. There was not the slightest probability that anybody would be looking for us - not right now and not for the rest of the day. All we could do was sit it out and wait.

So, what the hell! Why not listen to Harry's bloody story, I was going to do it for the heck of it and it would go in one ear and out the other. I was not interested in his story, no matter what. To hell with it! But then, can you refuse the last wish of a dying man?

Hazel

She made me the ultimate present, the beauty of her virginal soul . . .
Memories . . .

Harry began talking, slowly at first, often searching for words. But as he went on he became more confident. Hesitation disappeared and instead Harry surprised me by being an eloquent narrator, delivering his story with feeling and in a compelling, captivating manner.

The most memorable event of my life happened when I was a mere sixteen years old and has to do with my beautiful cousin Hazel, who was then just turning twenty. It started rather undramatically. My home-room teacher had sent a note of complaint to my mother. The outcome of that was that Hazel volunteered to give me a few private lessons after school. So I was instructed to go to the guesthouse, where she could keep an eye on me while doing her yoga exercises."

Harry paused. Then he gave me a searching look, as if he wanted to find out whether I approved of what he was saying, like a kid at school who had plucked up his courage to stand up in front of the class and start talking and was now getting scared to go on. But I only nodded in his direction, signalling encouragement and the fact that I was listening. He fumbled around for a brief moment and then continued.

I was upset, furious, fuming with rage at having my time with the other boys reduced. After all, that was the one thing that mattered to me. When I showed up at the place, I shot off a few really dumb remarks in her direction, rather unkind, the sort of stuff you can expect from a boy of sixteen, thoughtless verbal atrocities. But she ignored my silly, immature behaviour with gentle dignity.

She invited me to sit down and took the aggression out of the atmosphere, which I had been carrying with me like a mediaeval suit of armour. Still quite resentful I got into my math assignment. She was somewhere behind me, doing her - as I thought stupid - yoga exercises and had placed me at a little table that stood at the foot of a large mirror on the wall. After a while of busily beavering away at some impossible mathematical problem, I felt lost. I also thought that things had got very quiet behind me.

By chance I looked up. In the mirror ahead and above I saw the most beautiful image my youngster's eyes had ever seen, a picture of such superb gentleness that I thought my heart would stop. There was Hazel, clad in unbelievably beautiful undergarments - or lingerie as I might say today.

Harry smiled, eyes closed, lost in his memories and far, far away.

She was standing perfectly still with her arms crossed above her head to take off her dress, but not really taking it off, merely hiding her head in it. After quickly turning away in utter embarrassment, I cautiously raised my eyes again. As she was not looking at me but rather keeping her head and thus her eyes hidden from my view I plucked up the courage to take another long look at this incarnation of beauty, an aesthetic delight. After what seemed like an eternity of spellbound contemplation there was the faintest sign that she was about to come out of her yoga, giving me warning and time to put my head, which had acquired the colour of purple, back into my little book. She simply dropped the dress back into hugging this most perfect human shape.

Her parting words rang in my ears like the sweetest music. 'Please, come back tomorrow.'

This repeated itself. She had selected different garments, just as beautiful as the first time but more enticing. She struck a different pose, which she held, this time without the head hidden in the dress, which lay on a chair. She looked away from me, revealing her shapely silhouette.

The next day escalated to a full exposure of her beautiful back, and the one after that was to be the ultimate climax and also, sadly, our last day together. After I had sat down at the table as usual, she asked me to lower my head. I sensed the whisper of silk, as it slides over a woman's body. As lightning pulsed through me, I felt the gentlest, most tender touch of her fingertips, caressing my head, my hair, my neck, until she finally and very, very gently turned my head and whatever was connected with it around, facing her, bare and naked as she was the day she was born. Then she hugged and caressed me, kissing the tears in my eyes, because the finality of the event had started to overpower me.

'You must go, my darling,' she whispered tenderly. 'I love you so very much.'

We never met again. The next day her parents took her to Chicago, where she was married *at gun point* to a man she despised, to whom she had been promised by her father. I was to learn later that a generous cash-injection into the father's faltering business by the son-in-law was involved. The marriage was exceedingly unhappy and short, for her untimely early death put an end to her ordeal, which undoubtedly it must have been.

Later, much, much later, I was able to render an account to myself of what actually happened between us. She had known what was coming her way. As the obedient daughter she saw no way out except to do one thing and one thing only, once: to surrender herself to the one man of all she knew, whom she regarded the most highly. It touches me that it was me, a kid of sixteen, a boy on the way to manhood. She surrendered herself to me, completely and without reservations. She made me the ultimate present, the beauty of her virginal soul.

When Harry had finished there followed a long silence. He did not say anything further and I was completely lost for words. To say that I was surprised would have been a dramatic understatement. I had expected all sorts of things, but not a display of tender and sincere emotions, judging by the way in which he had chosen his words and delivered his story. You could tell that he was more than telling it. He was part of it, reliving the events that he was talking about. I had got the man all wrong, as wrong as could be. I would need to think about that. And then a startling realisation hit me: Here was a grown-up man telling his own story as a sixteen-year old, still being that sixteen-year old, endowed with the knowledge, understanding and perceptiveness of the grown-up man.

Goddammit! I thought, the poor bastard, Harry is stuck in the past! We both remained silent for a long while. I envied Harry his lovely experience but could also see that it had put him in a corner. Being a man, he must have found it hard to bare his soul to me.

After a long pause, Harry continued and took me through the period that followed. It became evident that Hazel had a lot to answer for. As with every process of enlightenment, his encounter with Hazel had served to set in him an expectation, which he had subsequently found impossible to forget. As became clearer and clearer with the unravelling of his story, Hazel had completely filled out every little bit of space in him that would otherwise have been accessible to other women, so that they could have dazzled him and made him fall in love. Instead, every experience that came his way had to measure up against Hazel's superb image, which, as time went on, assumed divine qualities.

At school he turned increasingly into a loner, but his one superb and remarkable experience in life, his enamouring encounter with Hazel, remained without any tangible consequences. There was nothing to suggest that he was destined for a life out of the ordinary or if there was, it did not manifest itself in any outwardly noticeable effects. Whatever it was, he buried it in the seemingly bottomless pit of a fantasy world, completely disconnected from the actual, physical life he was leading.

Harry was born in Peoria, Illinois. I had a notion that Peoria was the very centre of American mediocrity, of course undeservedly so as in the case of most of these generalisations. But at the time I almost burst out laughing when he said it. I hope the good folk of Peoria can forgive me for that. Maybe I was associating things with something that I may have heard somewhere, a long time ago. I truly and honestly do not know why, unless somebody had placed Peoria in the Bible Belt for me when I had asked where it was.

After college and without ever renouncing his secret reverence for Hazel Harry had taken a job on Wall Street, married Sheryl, 'the girl next door', raised an average American family with 1.2 kids and 0.9 dogs and mortgaged a set of two-by-fours and plaster-board in the commuter belt. Sorry if I sound profane, but that is what it was, according to Harry's slightly cynical account. When he lost his lucrative bank job, his wife divorced him. Coming to the conclusion that he was still too young to drink himself to death, he had remembered his skills as a helicopter pilot, which was why he was now here.

Harry was really quite a nice guy with an open and friendly face. It is always difficult for me if not outright impossible to describe how a man might appear in the eyes of a woman, quite apart from the fact that I have often wondered what criteria women apply when they select their boyfriends or husbands. My more typical reaction usually is one of 'how can such a fine woman get involved with such a jerk?' But in Harry's case that did not apply. He was definitely the type that women looked at.

Twice, if necessary.

At the company some of the girls thought that Harry was a darling. What is more, they thought he was available. Pauline thought he was a sonofabitch and did not mind telling everybody so. At the last company Christmas party she had tried to snuggle up to him, making rather friendly overtures. Harry, obviously still shell-shocked from his divorce, which in material terms had cost him his Porsche Nine-Eleven, the house and a lot of money, was not even remotely interested in a new romance and announced in front of a large enough audience, albeit after having consumed countless Margaritas, that all women were evil and wicked bitches and made a point of telling the world what he thought they could and should do with themselves, which has to remain unmentioned. When Pauline had got perhaps a little closer to Harry than might have been called for, he had told her exactly that, leaving her fuming with rage.

"Rude bastard" was the first thing she managed to throw at him a fraction of a second ahead of a not so dry Martini, splashed over his astonished face and his Gucci shirt.

It occurred to me that maybe the reason why his encounter with Hazel was so fresh on his mind was that he increasingly saw her as a true angel, especially after his divorce. As she no longer dwelt among the living, she did of course not make any mistakes, committed no blunders, hurt no feelings. Harry was retreating behind an emotional defence line, denying access and withdrawing into a fantasy world of imagined memories of good-old-times.

Harry's marrying the 'girl-next-door' deserved some more in-depth attention but he wanted to change the subject, away from his failed marriage. Maybe the memories still hurt. He had aroused my curiosity and given the right moment he would have to tell me more.

Outside darkness had fallen again. Not that it mattered. It was still snowing just as hard as before. We really had not missed out on anything. But I was getting a little worn out from listening to Harry and suggested that it was enough for one day's confessions. I wanted to forget Harry, who had already settled back into his general brooding attitude of gloom and impending doom. I needed some time to think.

The Beautiful Black Eyes

The night before Day 3
"Why did you crash your airplane?" asked the dark-brown-black eyes.

I spent most of the night tossing and turning, not being able to tell most of the time whether I was awake or asleep. An image kept appearing before me of two friendly, dark-brown-black eyes, more black than brown and the somewhat blurred features of a face. The name Xola fused with the image, a total entity of vision and sound.

Then there was some commotion outside the cabin door. As I opened it I found myself face to face with the Xola wolf, no more than three feet away. She was flanked on either side by three of her wolves, which hung back a little, staggered in an arrow-shaped formation, each animal overlapping the other by about a foot. At the back of the group there were more wolves, bringing up the rear in a single line, six abreast and everybody was looking at me except three sentries, which had taken up positions in a semi-circle around the cabin and the pack of wolves in front of it, with their backs towards me and the pack, sitting on their haunches with heads high in the air, scanning the neighbourhood and the horizon for the slightest sign of danger.

I tried to go through the door towards the animals but could not move. Then I realised that it was still night and I had not left my bed, having woken up from a dream . . . it had promised to develop into something . . .

. . . maybe

. . . exciting

. . . tossing and turning

. . . darkness . . .

Then I was back with the Xola wolf and looked into beautiful brown-black eyes. She jumped right into a conversation and wanted to know about my plans, whether I was going to remain living in Wolfland.

"No, no," I assured her. "My friend and I have no plans to stay. Soon some people will come from our base and take us back. It's just a matter of a few days."

"And if they don't come?" The beautiful eyes with a lovely sparkle in them looked at me with serious concern, hoping to hear something positive, so that she would not have to worry about us.

"They will, they always do. That's part of our way of life." I tried to sound as convincing and at the same time as casual as possible, to be able to move away from this subject quickly . . .

. . . again I was wide awake and sitting upright on my bed. Maybe I had been toying with ideas in a half-sleep and the thought shot through my head that the company would be much better off not finding me. I was not at all convinced that they would carry on a sustained search-and-rescue operation, once they had a good enough reason to call it off and collect the insurance, something like $300,000 for the old Beaver, daylight robbery if you ask me, and another $500,000 on my head as key-man-insurance for loss of operational earnings while looking for my successor. What a truly comforting thought: I was worth half a million – dead.

I dismissed the idea straight away – no, our people wouldn't do such a thing. I was convinced that they would put in a determined effort and pull out all the stops to get us back. But the mind is a strange beast, obviously capable of pursuing ideas of its own, 'uncontrolled mental ramblings', as our philosophy teacher in high school once put it.

More tossing and turning, longing to go back to sleep . . .

"Why did you crash your airplane?" asked the brown-black eyes.

"I did not really crash it. The rough landing was not intentional. I landed the plane all right but then it just broke, the engine had stopped working. Without power I could not keep the aircraft in the air, so it went down and I tried to avoid the worst."

"You could not have gone on flying?"

"No, not another fifty yards. If you like, I landed it where there was no place to land - to stop it from falling out of the sky, like a dead bird."

I should not have said that, for it prompted a sharp-tongued response.

"Well, if it had been a bird, somebody would eat it, and after a while nothing would be left of it. But your airplane will be an eyesore for a long time to come."

"When the ice melts, in the summer, it will drop to the ocean floor and disappear." Mr. Smartass was charging headlong through a china shop.

"And poison the fish and all the other creatures in the sea." Ms. Lady Wolf looked at me with every sign of reproach in her brown-black eyes.

"I see, we have us a little green crusader here, do we?"

"I am merely showing concern for the world we live in, my world, our world. It is your world too."

Of course, she was absolutely right. What excuse did we have to leave a burnt-out pile of junk in the middle of otherwise unspoiled nature? I could see her point and so thought it was only appropriate that I should offer remedial action. "As soon as possible I shall come back with a couple of guys and a truck and we'll take what's left of it back to base."

That softened her slightly agitated mood a little bit, but the inquisitive phase of our meeting was not yet over.

"Why did you fly through the air? We keep seeing your airplanes going back and forth. What is the reason for that activity?" asked the eyes.

"Basically," I was trying to find something that she could easily relate to, so I did not mention spare parts and machine tools, "we have people in a camp a little further to the north and we have to bring them food or they would starve to death." I thought I was pretty clever. This would end the argument.

"They don't find food where they live?"

"No."

"Then they should go away, somewhere else, where they find food. It does not make sense to fly food through the air, unless you are a bird, feeding your young ones in the nest."

"It's not that simple. The people there drill for oil, hidden deep under the surface. Then they put it in the pipeline and pump it to the loading terminal, from where ships take it away."

"And what do you need the oil for?"

"Well," Mr. Smartass was obviously still in top form and doing overtime, "among other things we need it to fly our aircraft."

". . . which you would not need to do if the people weren't drilling for oil in a place where they don't find anything to eat, so they need airplanes to bring them food, which need oil for the engines so that they can fly. This is not even funny."

She was absolutely right. The exchange went on for a little longer. I am cutting it short for only one reason. No matter what I said, she replied with logic or common sense that was clearly of a higher order. It was almost impossible to defend our Western civilisation in a way that you could sell to a wolf.

"Listen, Jack," she locked her beautiful eyes squarely on to mine, "I don't want to sound cantankerous or argumentative, but these things are vital to us wolves, they touch on our very existence. Before you, the white people, came, there were the Indians and us, the animals. Both sides respected one another, giving each other space to live. The Indians called us their brothers and sisters. They cared about us. Wolf and Indian lived side by side, for hundreds of years, both content, neither eager to change things. Now things change from one day to the next and it is not getting better. That is all I have to say."

This rather definitive statement from her would mark the end of the formal part of the meeting.

She relaxed visibly and turned her head to look first over her right, then her left shoulder, obviously a signal to her escort. Its somewhat military formation dissolved. While only the sentries stayed on duty everybody else made themselves comfortable, settling down on the ground in groups of twos and threes. There was a pleasant social atmosphere of friendly banter and subdued conversation. It reminded me of my last visit to Paris and the *Café de la Paix* the atmosphere, the complete absence of any aggression and the relaxed disregard for the passage of time.

Xola lowered her athletic body to the ground and I crouched down in front of her, sitting on a log of firewood that I had got from inside the cabin. We could now talk informally and the most obvious subject on her mind was family and the relations that each of us had. I got the ball rolling by inquiring about her topwolf, to whom she had referred as Gonzo. I asked where he was and why he had not come along. That surprised her because she thought I knew that a topwolf has a twenty-four-hours-a-day-job defending the realm, patrolling the perimeter and the terrain to seek out and chase away or bring to heel intruders and take possession of any female wolves that strayed onto the patch, to induct them in the pack.

"Are you jealous of all the other wolves?" I asked her.

"No, why should I be? That is part of our culture, our heritage. I grew up with that. I was educated to become the first lady of a pack and that's what I am: ambition fulfilled, I'm happy, couldn't ask for more."

I was embarrassed for having thrown my preconceived notions about the relationship of the sexes right at her.

"We are one large happy family. Everybody has rights and duties and accepts them with pleasure."

I was never able to say with certainty whether dogs could smile; the same would be true for wolves, but I thought that she was smiling now.

"You have a pack of your own?" she asked.

"Well, of sorts. I've got one wife and two kids, the kids are grown up and the wife and I don't live together."

"Why not?"

"Well, actually, we are divorced."

"What's that?" Xola looked at me with a mixture of suspicion and concern.

"It means that we are no longer one family that lives together."

"How sad."

"Not really," I replied, "that's what I am used to."

"How can you live alone? That is unnatural. Don't you need somebody for warmth, affection and company?"

"Yes, I really think I do, but it just doesn't work out that way."

"But you have mistresses?" She looked at me expectantly.

"I'm afraid I don't." I was embarrassed, for in her eyes I must have looked like a complete failure.

"You should have three," she said, pausing for an instant before she added, "three and a wife."

"Three what?"

"Mistresses. That would be good for you and good for your women. No woman can bear and tolerate the full-time presence of a man; it's better to spread the load. If you have only one mistress she will compete with your wife, two will gang up against her, but three will try to be good friends amongst them and with everybody, including the wife."

"Six! You should have six!" One of the female wolves on her right had moved forward a little and tried to get in on the conversation.

"Shut up, Joumana, nobody asked you!"

Xola snarled at one of her escorts, baring her teeth with unmistakable emphasis, looking genuinely fierce and threatening. Joumana simply flicked up her chin defiantly and was not overly frightened or impressed. Xola turned back towards me, all sweetness and charm again. I sensed that she and Joumana were really good friends, putting on this little number just for me, to make fun of me. So I showed myself to be suitably impressed, which in turn made the two wolves put their heads together, as if they were exchanging secrets, giggling like schoolgirls.

"Maybe you're right. But our women are not conditioned for that. They want all of one man. They do not want to share him."

"But do they give all of themselves, all the time?"

Xola had put her finger or paw rather, right on it.

She wanted to know more about the subject of divorce and was shocked by what I had told her. So I explained that almost a third of marriages end prematurely in divorce.

"Our model of marriage has a high failure rate. We have a Consumer Protection Agency. If we buy something of which about a third does not work we can make a claim for damages and get our money back or a replacement. Yet with marriage breaking down nothing of the sort happens. People get married again and again, but we still hold on to our system as being the only true and acceptable form. Co-habitation, just living together, is merely tolerated with reservations."

The wolves were shocked. It meant that our, the human society, had no truly reliable and sustainable model for creating a family or 'pack', as Xola put it.

Joumana was steadily inching her way forward to listen in and was not in the least concerned about respecting Xola's privacy and mine. Then Xola wanted to give me a full account of how the subject is handled in Wolfland.

Basically, it starts with one ambitious male. First he will look around for a territory as his 'home patch'. It may not be difficult to find but is usually occupied by another wolf. In order to acquire his land he needs to be chased away or killed if he fails to follow a serious invitation to leave. With territory our wolf has now also acquired the status of topwolf. He can now form a pack of his own. The first thing he does is find a few females. They may be accompanied by youngsters and the boys can stay as long as they don't get in the way of the topwolf. Once they feel the urge they either beat the hell out of him and take over the pack or go away elsewhere to start their own and then it starts all over. The wolves in the pack will work out their seniority system. One of them will emerge as the female lead wolf. She will be the strongest, most beautiful and most desirable female in the pack and will be the only one allowed to give birth to offspring to add to the pack.

When she and only she thinks the time is right topwolf will get an unmistakable summons to rush to her side, whereupon he will briefly interrupt the hunting down and chasing away or killing of intruders. He will then submit himself to his lady by lying on his back, exposing his throat to her deadly bite, inviting her to kill him.

If she does not kill him it usually means that she loves him and they sneak off to a secluded spot to do it. After that topwolf goes back to the business of the day and she nurses the fruit in her body.

The other females in the pack cuddle up to her and each other for warmth and comfort. A female that does not make it to first lady may never bear and raise cubs; natural selection of the strongest and fittest, of course. When topwolf gets tired of the job he will stand down and retire and take with him some of the older females whom he will entertain generously as his mistresses. This is the real fun part. No cares. No worries, just fun and games, interrupted occasionally by more fun and games - heaven on earth.

Everybody is happy. The species is continued in the best possible way; the young wolves are happy with each other and Ms. first lady without having to worry about getting pregnant. Perhaps the unlucky ones are the surplus males that do not make it to topwolf. But then every system has to have its checks and balances and, all things considered, this must be one of the better systems. They have no religion, which helps a lot. For that reason, divorce is unknown; child support is everybody's obligation and all a man has to do is to become topwolf and do the two things that he is good at, hunt-and-kill and the other, whatever that was.

That – I have condensed it a bit - was the way Xola described their system and society to me.

"Now I want to hear all about your society and the human way of life." Xola looked at me expectantly.

"And so do I," added Joumana eagerly, as she cleverly manoeuvred herself between Xola and me. There was no avoiding it. I had to give them as good an account as I could.

"Well, come to think of it, I guess our way of doing things also begins with an ambitious male, one that starts looking for a soul mate." The wolves were amused, as they crept up ever so much closer, so as not to miss a word. All the female wolves in the pack had moved up and were listening with undivided attention.

"The men chase the women, and the women run away."

"But if that were so, they would never meet?" Joumana asked innocently.

"Well, actually, they appear to run away, but in reality they don't. They need to get the man's attention, so that he will come after them. Once he does, things change. She reverses her tactics, gives him the hot-and-cold treatment. One moment she oozes charm and sex appeal, the next she plays hard to get."

"Jack, aren't you being cynical? We want the truth, not some goose story that you are cooking up because you may harbour a deeply rooted grudge against women." Xola gave me a stern look.

"Is it that obvious?" I put surprise into my voice.

"I'm afraid so; the truth, Jack, nothing but the truth."

"Well, men have a natural urge to chase women and once they've caught them they want to get rid of them. Women, on the other hand, set traps to catch a man, but once they've got him they want to lock him up, throw away the key and keep him, like in a safe deposit box."

"What's that?" said Joumana.

"It's a box in which people keep things dear to them, like money."

The wolves were horrified.

"What an awful way to live." Xola was visibly disturbed.

". . . yeah, if he's telling the truth." Joumana was not convinced at all. "Listen, Jack, let's just have the bare bones of the facts."

"Yeah, with a little meat on them," added one of the other wolves who had moved up with the rest of the pack. That must have been the closest thing to a wolf joke imaginable and I was sure they were all roaring inwardly with laughter.

"OK, people, these are the hard facts. It looks like Nature made a mistake. The men have the urge to survive and the urge to screw women." I did not mean to put it so crudely, but the wolves did not mind one tiny bit. On the contrary, they all nodded their heads in appreciation and with obvious approval when I said it, so I went on. "Meanwhile, the women are endowed with the power of sexual attraction. They attract men in numbers and then select the one that gives them the best deal."

"What do you mean by best deal?" Xola was now as alert and attentive as anybody ever could be.

"She goes for the guy with the largest patch, the best hunting grounds, to put it into *WolfSpeak*." I was not comfortable with this part of the conversation.

"What about the personality side of things? Doesn't that matter?" Joumana was concerned.

"Well, yes, that does matter. Of all the nice guys she chooses the one nice guy with the largest patch."

"Girls," Joumana looked around, "this man's story is not all that different from ours. There isn't a thing in what he said that you wouldn't somehow find in Wolfland. It's just how the whole thing is connected that's different."

"Yeah, they have all the right urges, but don't know how to sort things out properly, right?" Xola looked around for approval, only to see a general affirmative nodding of heads. Turning towards me she added: "There is nothing wrong with your urges. It's just what you do with them, how you react, whether you follow your inner voice for guidance or whether you live against your own self."

"Yeah, how true."

"True . . . true . . . true." There was general murmur of approval.

"So what do we do wrong?" I looked at them, my eyes wandering from one to the other.

"You simply have to reconcile your lifestyle with your natural dispositions and endowments. Once you do that you'll be fine, Jack, just like us."

"How do you always know what to do? How do you recognise your natural dispositions? I'm sure that is the fine art of living." I must have sounded a bit dejected, when I said that and I certainly felt that way. So Xola was quick to cheer me up.

"You have to be like us, figure out what it is that you have to do to lead a happy and fulfilled life and make it part of your society's philosophy."

"Our society has a lot of philosophies, but none of them work. We don't have any clear and ready answers for how to get through life happily. What is it that makes your philosophy so successful?"

"Truthfulness, honesty, living in harmony with your inner self and the fundamental dispositions that you harbour within you. There are a number of very basic and simple facts of life, a little more than a dozen. If you understand those and live by them you will be successful. We call ours our Credo, our life's philosophy."

"I would give a lot to know your Credo. Maybe it will give answers to some things that have bothered me all my life. I would like to know what makes your society tick."

"Tick?" Xola looked puzzled.

"Well, work. When something works well, we say it ticks."

"The wolf pack certainly ticks, there is no doubt about it. We are all getting along great, everything runs smoothly and everyone is happy."

"So it's because of your Credo?" I must have sounded a bit sceptical.

"Well, perhaps it's more like our Credo explaining why things work so well."

"You've got me all curious. Come on, let's hear it, let me hear your Wolf-Pack-Credo." I was eager to find out about the wolves' great mystery. That must have impressed Xola. She turned to Joumana. "You can recite it from memory, can't you, Joumana?"

"Can't everybody?" Joumana responded a bit pompously, but then she was happy about a little bit of centre-stage action.

"Right, here it is, our *Wolf-Pack-Credo.* It consists of fifteen *Maxims*:

1. *Think positively*
2. *Follow your instincts*
3. *Believe in yourself and your abilities*
4. *Trust your own judgment*
5. *Remember that you always have three choices*

Come on, don't let me do all the work!" She turned to the other wolves: "What are the choices?" She looked around like a platoon sergeant checking up on how well the soldiers knew the drill, eliciting a chorus of voices from some of the other wolves:

- *"To do nothing*
- *To do something or*
- *To do something else"*

"Excellent!" Joumana beamed at the platoon. "Let me go on:

6. *When in doubt what to do – do nothing*
7. *Never give someone a choice between something and nothing; make it a choice between something and something else, otherwise you get nothing*
8. *What defies rational explanation is probably not true*
9. *The truth will always come out, sooner or later*
10. *When in need you will discover that there are three kinds of friends:*

Well, people, your turn again," and she faced the other wolves that had stepped in before:

- *"Those who have to rush off on urgent business*
- *Those who give good advice*
- *Those who help"*

"Exactly! And here is the rest:

11. *Don't lose sleep over yesterday's problems, you did that yesterday*
12. *The sun always shines – sometimes we just cannot see it*
13. *It is never over until it is over*
14. *There is always a way out*
15. *Courage wins!"*

Joumana clearly enjoyed her little performance and she had said the last three *Maxims* with great emphasis.

"Thank you, Joumana; that was very impressive." Xola gave her a glance of approval. "So now you know all about the magic that makes a wolf-pack work the way it does, my friend. But – to use your own words – your airplane did not tick, did it?" Xola obviously wanted to tease me.

"Xola, do you have to remind me? Well, the answer is no, our aircraft did not tick."

Xola was completely at ease. "The wolf pack certainly ticks."

The conversation had reached its logical conclusion and the pack got ready to leave. The escort regrouped, without a word having been spoken or orders being barked. They just knew what to do. We exchanged the appropriate courtesies on parting with kindest and most sincere regards for our respective partners and family. Xola obviously and, I believe, in deliberate disapproval, ignored the fact that I had said that I lived alone. The somewhat formal goodbye culminated in an assurance of best wishes and utmost concern for one another's health and well being and that of our families.

Before she turned to go Xola looked at me with what I thought was another smile and said, "Get some mistresses! It's fun for everybody." With that she turned around and walked through the escort, who did an about face to march her out. The sentries took up forward and flanking positions and once they had covered a certain distance the pack settled into its normal working formation with Xola leading from the front and everybody joining up in a throng around and behind her.

When I woke up daylight was seeping through the shutters. I went outside to check the weather. As I stood in the open door, I could see a wolf pack as it disappeared behind a large mound. So they were around, somewhere. And then I had the startling thought that it was strange for me to fantasise about a wolf-woman with beautiful brown-black eyes. Why her, why not Yuko?

I made a point of checking our surroundings for any sign of a rescue effort that had been launched in our direction. I climbed a little hill next to the cabin, which improved my height above terrain by about thirty feet and gave me a good view all the way to the mountains. As hard as I looked I could not see any sign of an aircraft in the sky nor could I hear anything that sounded like an aircraft engine, be it chopper or fixed wing. If they were out there, and I was absolutely sure they were, they would be too far away for us to see or hear them from where we were.

Today was the first day since our disappearance that flying was possible, if you wanted to be able to see the ground, looking for somebody. There would be an aircraft out there, doing a search pattern, maybe even more than one. They would start with the position that Harry had last radioed through and would probably be horrified, thinking that we might have hit a mountain or plunged into one of the crevasses. I thought they would give it all day. If they found nothing by the end of it they would sit down and reconsider the situation. Somebody would look at a copy of the flight plan which I had filed and the series of crosses on the grid map up to the last one at N06/201 M06/202, as called in by Harry. That would give them the distance from our point of departure. Then they would add about twenty minutes' worth of flying and do two circles from the first way-point as per my flight plan. Once they did that they should put my original flight plan on the grid map and ask themselves why I hadn't stuck to it or what was different or what went wrong.

That would eventually give them an area of about fifty by thirty miles, which is not really such an awful lot, once you decide that that is where you want to go looking. The people at base were not stupid and if I was able to think of it, so were they. Sooner or later they would find us. Probably not today, while they were checking up on Harry's last reported position plus twenty minutes, actually eighteen, if we had crashed when the next call was due. I found all that quite reassuring.

Yes, I thought, this will be just a matter of time.

But what if they did not think that way? What if they really thought we were lost somewhere in the depth of a crevasse? Could we just go on sitting here, doing nothing?

Operations

"Maybe we're overlooking something here." Slowly working it out . . . .

"They're dead." Hank Snyder dropped into a chair near the door in Operations, exhausted. Yesterday, all day long, they had been in a constant state of readiness, but unable to go on account of the storm and the dense and low cloud cover, making visual aircraft operations in the search area impossible. Today had been a different story. Scott Raleigh flying the Otter and Hank Snyder in the Huey had taken off at first light, heading straight for the position last reported by Harry. On finding nothing they had started their search in continuing the assumed flight path of the missing aircraft. Within less than fifteen minutes it had become apparent that something was very wrong. Terrain height increased, making it impossible to continue on the assumed course without crashing the chopper into the side of a mountain range that rose to above eight thousand feet. Of course, they had seen this on the map but had wanted to check it out 'for real', to make sure they were not missing some important clue.

After a brief consultation over the radio between base and Scott Raleigh in the Twin Otter and Hank Snyder in the Huey they agreed on a search pattern, which extended to about ten miles on either side of the straight-line flight path. The Huey went back to base twice for fuel, the Otter once. At the end of the day they had looked into every nook and cranny, circled around every rock outcrop and looked down into ravines as much as they had dared, without seeing so much as a trace of the missing aircraft and its crew. If the aviators were alive, they would certainly see the rescue aircraft and try to signal their whereabouts in whatever way possible. But there had been nothing to suggest that anybody was trying to signal the rescuers.

"Maybe we're overlooking something here." Teresa Sullivan was staring a hole into the grid map on the table. "What was their visibility at that time?"

She got annoyed looks from some of the men present for daring to offer an opinion on an aviation matter that she could not possibly know anything about, apart from the fact that she was a woman. No chauvinism intended, but this was man's country. Women darned the socks and cooked the beans. But Teresa was not in the least discouraged.

"Well?"

"It was bad, low cloud cover. According to Harry they were at about a thousand feet above terrain, with the base of the clouds right above them." Collins was the one to know if anybody did, for he had talked to Harry.

"So, they would have flown bang against the side of the hill and we should have seen them or what's left of them and the Beaver. But there was nothing. Not a thing. They were never there." Teresa looked up from the map. "Why are we so sure they would be at the end of this pencil line?"

The first reactions were some angry looks. Then Bob Masters said, "Yeah, the girl is right, why the hell are we?" And after a pause he added, "Who did the calling in, Jack or Harry?"

"Harry." Collins looked tired. It was not just from not having slept for two days and nights save for a few hours here and there. He felt the weight of responsibility. Above all, he should have taken a closer look when Harry called in the positions; especially the last one or two, setting a course smack against the side of the mountain, which he should have seen and challenged, asked to clarify, advised of the danger that he saw. But he had never looked closely at the positions that were reported to him and hence had not noticed anything. As a result, he had done nothing. Well, Jack never needed any babysitter, he thought, trying to justify to himself his lack of action.

"All the calls?" Masters persisted.

"Yeah, all of them, the whole damned lot of them, except the first one, which was the way-point after leaving Bravo. Jack called that in himself." Collins was angry.

"You know, looking at this line, you would have thought that Jack wanted to commit suicide. It's pretty damned obvious that they were bound to run into the side of the mountain. But he never appeared in the least bit suicidal to me." Masters was not finished yet. "You look at that string of entries on the grid map and you get the most perfect straight line. That's not the flying of a man who's lost."

"Yeah, I second that. Besides, he booked a seat on tomorrow's mail flight to Anchorage. You reckon he would commit suicide first and then go to the big city for some R & R?" Paul Baxter remembered taking the reservation.

"And he's got a luncheon appointment, wouldn't say who with." Masters made his contribution.

"Well, OK, let's rule out suicide and murdering Harry, although," Collins hesitated and a faint, wicked smile crossed his face, "I've been tempted to do that myself, at times."

"You said it, Bill." Masters also managed a smile, despite the gravity of the situation. "What if that line is all wrong? We know the point of origin and it's spot on to the first way-point, because we logged the radar fix transmitted from Camp Bravo before they drove out of range. What happened after that? Why don't we look at Jack's flight plan?"

"Should have done that long ago, for Chrissake . . ." Masters muttered more to himself, while Collins was already marking the second way-point, as per the flight plan.

"Shit, do you see what I see?" The second line comfortably missed the mountain by about five miles. "We know the man was flying absolutely straight, Harry couldn't have made that up. There must be some fundamental mistake in the positions that were called in. What if Harry got it all wrong?"

"With Jack listening in, saying nothing? Hank Snyder was not convinced.

" . . . you ever flown in our Beaver? That thing is as noisy inside the cockpit as a machine shop on a busy day. It would be easy not to hear what someone said into a mike." Scott Raleigh was talking from experience, having been the last person to fly the Beaver before the ferry flight.

"Well," Collins took control of the situation, "maybe Teresa has got something there. Let's re-plan this thing for tomorrow morning. If the weather plays ball we'll re-enact Jack's flight plan."

Time to Remember, Time to Think

Day 4
"What have I done?" Harry, after his wedding

The fourth day looked like it did not want to start at all. It was pitch dark inside the cabin and almost as dark outside. Thick black clouds were rising from the ground. Snow came down heavily. But the darkness also made us less aware of the desolation and loneliness of the place. I found it most remarkable that at some time someone actually lived here, whoever built the cabin.

This was one of those days when you do not feel like getting out of bed. Fixing tea suddenly looked like a brilliant idea. I forgot to mention the biscuit tin with the picture of the three puppies outside and the screw-on top, which was filled with teabags.

"Say, Harry, fancy a spot of tea?" I wanted to cheer him up a little, break down that wall of brooding silence, behind which he retreated, whenever he was not telling me another part of his life's tragedy. He looked up at me, surprised.

"A spot of tea? You English are a funny bunch. The last time I heard that expression was in some black-and-white movie."

"I'm British, Harry, not English. My mother was French, born in Marseille, my father was from Edinburgh, as Scottish as they come and I was born a British citizen in Mombasa, Kenya, when it was still a British Colony and just before the outbreak of the Mau-Mau Uprising."

"Wow, I'm impressed." Harry was making an effort to demonstrate that he was again among the living. For a moment he looked lost in thought. Maybe he had simply forgotten what he had started out saying. Then he got back into it, adding, "I still don't see why you're not English. Your Queen is English."

"That's actually open to some debate. Some bad people out there say that your mother and father and their mothers and fathers have to be English to be able to call yourself English. The Queen might have a problem with that. Anyway, we are all Brits."

"Yeah, why argue?" Harry managed a hint of a smile. "English, British, who gives a rat's ass anyway when we'll soon be dead and eaten by your wolves?"

He had snapped back into his dark mood, but I knew now that I could pull him out of it if I kept on talking to him, making him do things and giving him less time to feel sorry for himself. After we had finished our tea we settled back into our previous activities, that is to say we continued to do nothing. The weather made it quite unnecessary to come up with any excuses why we were not busy as beavers. There simply was nothing that we could have done, either in or outside the cabin. So we both just remained there, lying on our bunks, each of us following his thoughts.

Nothing dramatic was going to happen today. One look outside the door had convinced me that in such foul weather there would be no rescue flights. And it most certainly did not look like any change for the better was imminent. On the contrary, it kept on getting worse. That was the perfect moment for getting on with listening to Harry. My initial resistance to it and rejection of the very thought had given way to acute and sincere interest, fuelled by equally acute and sincere curiosity.

"Say, Harry, why *did* you marry Sheryl?" I wanted to use the time to get to the bottom of Harry's story. "After what you told me about Hazel and what you still felt for her it is hard to think of that as having been a passionate love affair."

Harry looked up, surprised. At first I thought he would react angrily, for my question was an intrusion into his privacy. But the contrary was the case.

"You don't mind me asking?" I didn't want to upset him.

"No, no, not at all, I'm actually glad that you mention it. Ever since I've started telling you my story I have been thinking about nothing else. I am asking myself again and again why I really did marry her."

No further encouragement was needed. Harry jumped right into it. As I had suspected all along he had stumbled into his marriage. After college he first came back to his hometown, stayed at his parents' house and worked for one of the local banks. Sheryl meanwhile had finished her formal education at the City College and was now teaching little kiddies at grade school. As they were next door neighbours it was unavoidable that she and Harry came face to face often, sometimes more than once on the same day. But Sheryl gave him the cold shoulder treatment. An occasional 'hi!' from her was about as good as things got.

This changed dramatically when he was spotted by a head-hunter and got the New York job. Thanksgiving was the first time he came back home for a few days. After his parents had picked him up at the airport he asked them to drop him off at Freddie's Sports Car Emporium, where he collected his brand new Porsche Nine-Eleven. This deal had been long in the making. While he still worked at the local bank, his credit rating had been insufficient to support such an acquisition. The Wall Street job had brought a fifty per cent salary increase over what the local bank had paid him. But that was not enough to explain the sudden change of financial as well as social climate with which Harry met wherever he went. The New York job had meant an enormous boost to his image. The most noteworthy change could be observed in Sheryl's attitude towards him. The cryptic 'hi!' had given way to an enthusiastic and warm welcome.

"Hey, Harry, great to see you again, say, you look smart." And she had put her left arm around him in a little hug, to give him a kiss on the cheek. Harry was both confused at this sudden change of attitude and surprised. But he did not mind. It made him feel good. He enjoyed the attention, of which there was more to come.

Listening to him I thought a little cynically that overnight by changing jobs and hanging out with the big boys in the big city his status had without any transition or warning transformed itself from that of lone wolf to top dog. Now things were happening on a broad front. First his parents started 'thinking aloud', how nice it would be to have grandchildren before they themselves got too old to hold them in their laps. Then his sister suggested that he ought to 'make his move', before he 'missed the bus'. By 'sheer coincidence' he was dragged along to two weddings in quick succession. Then Sheryl's parents asked the whole family over for 'afternoon tea', which they had never done before, and 'wasn't it just wonderful to have such charming neighbours'.

That afternoon Harry asked Sheryl to go out with him in the evening. After the meal and an action thriller at the Fox Alhambra they wound up at Ralph's Piano Bar, where Sheryl made her move. In addition to being more than pretty to look at she was a smart dresser and had a gorgeous body, which she wrapped around Harry whenever there was a slow number and they danced. Needless to say, all the music at Ralph's was of the slow-motion seductive type.

Harry suddenly felt the urge. Holy smoke, what a woman, he thought. How could I have overlooked her for so long! Well, of course he had not really. Sheryl had turned into a different woman, because she had wanted to. She had pulled out all the stops and it was beginning to work. On the way home he pulled the Porsche over in a secluded spot that he knew from his high school days as 'necking alley'. He just could not hold back any more. As he kissed her passionately he found himself cursing his 'damn'd foreign import' with the stick shift and the central tunnel between him and Sheryl that stood in the way of serious lovemaking. What he would have given at that moment for a good old classic American sedan from the fifties with a front bench seat and a column shift, like the old '53 Chevy which he drove as a student.

But he need not have worried, for it would not have made any difference. As his hand tenderly caressed its way upwards between her thighs from the lovely feeling of stockings to the even lovelier feeling of bare skin to within a fraction of an inch from reaching paradise a metallic voice suddenly said NO!'

Harry could not believe it. Had this woman no heart?

"Harry, we cannot do something like that, we hardly know each other." Sheryl looked at him with big, innocent eyes. "This isn't New York, you know. These are all respectable citizens around us, and we have to behave ourselves. After all, in a few days you will be going back and leave me here to dream about that wonderful man from the big city, while you make all those New York girls happy. Besides, I have to be able to look my parents in the eye. And" she added, giving him a long, serious look, "I am a school teacher and have to maintain a certain moral standard. You know what this town is like, Harry, you grew up here. Have you forgotten everything?"

Harry had forgotten nothing. He knew exactly what people would say and think. His hand came travelling back again, from the naked thigh to the stocking and into the devastating nothingness of having to let go of his object of desire, which was what Sheryl had become. At the door she put up a slow and reluctant struggle as if trying not to get hugged and kissed, allowing him enough contact to know what he would be missing.

"See you tomorrow?" He asked with a lump in his throat.

"Of course, dummy, remember, we've got the potluck lunch at the church." After all, it was Thanksgiving.

"You know, about New York . . ." he hesitated and then he had said it. Like a bullet that has left the barrel of the gun, the words had been irretrievably uttered: "Why don't you come with me to New York?"

"As what, your mistress?" Sheryl knew how to bring a man to his knees.

"No, no." Harry was on the brink of surrender. "You know how I meant the question."

"Well, if that is what you are trying to tell me, why don't you come out and say it?"

His hands had slid down on to her buttocks, pressing her body firmly against his, which she pretended not to notice. A mixture of joy, lust, desire and despair had come over him, as the urge took a firm hold of him and switched the supply of blood from his brains to the lower part of his body, where, temporarily, it was more effective.

"You want to be my . . ." Harry was groping for words, could not finish the sentence.

"I know what you are trying to say to me. How sweet, Harry." She rewarded him with a long, sensual kiss. "See you tomorrow, darling." Before he could do anything further, Sheryl had slipped out of his arms and through the door, pulling it shut behind her.

That night Harry did not sleep a wink. It was torture. The red monster of desire had firmly taken hold of him; the mortal wound had been inflicted. All it would take now would be a gentle nudge with the fingertips to topple Harry over.

It came the next afternoon, after his and Sheryl's families had come back from the community function at the church and assembled at his parents' house to get ready for Thanksgiving dinner. As they were all getting seated around the table, Harry next to Sheryl, Harry's mother put the finishing touches to the unwitting conspiracy.

"I hear you and Sheryl want to tell us something?" She looked around with an expression of triumph and delight on her face.

"How exciting," was the general comment all around, while everybody's eyes had started drilling holes into poor Harry.

"Well . . ." Harry got up from his chair, not really knowing why, slowly buttoned up his jacket, put his napkin on the table and said – nothing.

"Come on, darling, tell them," nudged Sheryl, "tell them, you know . . ."

"Oh my dear, are you?" Harry's mother had jumped up from her chair and come around to put her arms around Harry and Sheryl, who had also got up.

"How absolutely wonderful! The children are getting married! You are, Harry, aren't you?"

"Yes, mother," whispered Harry almost inaudibly, not really knowing what he was saying.

Sheryl let out a shriek of triumph, hugging first Harry, then his mother, then her mother, then jumping up and down, hugging Harry again and everybody else. There was mayhem in the dining room of the Parker house, total chaos. Everybody was congratulating everybody else. Harry received more backslapping than in the decade before, while the women eagerly discussed the event, the pitch of their voices getting higher and higher, the more the significance of it had started to hit home. Before the family turkey had managed to find its way onto the plates of Harry and his family and their guests Harry had set in motion the wheels of disaster that were to lead up to the biggest turkey of his life. Before the evening was over he and Sheryl were engaged. It was his father who finally put the noose inescapably around his neck.

"So, what are we looking at here? You're engaged, son, right?"

"Of course they are, dear," volunteered Harry's mother.

"Let the man speak for himself. Son, you want to go on record?"

Everybody's eyes were on Harry again.

"Yes." Harry almost choked to death, trying to utter that one little word. That was all he ever said. But it was enough. There was another howl of triumph from Sheryl, which really should have warned Harry that he was about to enter the road of no return and potential tragedy. Alas, that is easier said than done and shares the fate of famous last words and unheeded premonitions. It is all crystal clear afterwards, when even the notorious blind man can see it, but at the time, when it had happened, Harry had been unaware that he was about to commit an enormous blunder.

It is amazing what a woman will do and get done in next to no time if she wants to. Somehow the 'paperwork' was miraculously completed, masterminded and expedited by Sheryl. I actually wondered whether in the State of Illinois you can get married from one day to the next. In many states and countries they have to put your name up on a board and inform the world what is in the offing. But Harry never referred to that and I did not want to ask. After all, they did get married.

On Saturday they exchanged the vows at the church. Over the rest of that fateful weekend Sheryl generously rewarded Harry with all the pleasures that her shapely body was capable of delivering, if instructed to do so by its owner. For Harry it was the first and last really good sex that he would encounter in his relationship with Sheryl. On Monday Sheryl Parker was sitting in the right seat of the Porsche, as she and her husband were heading east on Interstate 80.

For those few days Hazel had not once intruded in Harry's thoughts. Halfway to New York she was back and recriminations started setting in. As the blood, no longer needed in the lower regions, returned to the brains, so did Hazel and with her the thinking process, culminating in Harry's words 'what have I done?'

This was followed by the depressing insight that he found himself chained to a woman whom he had desired sexually, albeit briefly and under the compelling weight of circumstances, but did not love.

Harry was realistic. Sheryl was a good catch, as catches go. She was pretty to look at, well spoken, had nice manners and many other attributes that had so endeared her to Harry's mother. But it was not love on Sheryl's side either and Harry could feel it. Sheryl was pushing twenty-five and did not want to wind up an old spinster, as she had confided in Harry's sister. Love had passed her by, not that she did not get a lot of attention. It was the wrong kind of attention. And then, all of a sudden, the Lord had answered her prayers for a good, respectable husband. Harry was a Wall Street banker! That was about as good as it could get in her way of thinking. She had already made a conscious decision not to wind up with a schoolteacher for a husband. Harry had been the last 'good' man to cross her path and Harry had been available.

You cannot blame Sheryl for what she did. That was perfectly normal feminine behaviour. It was just tough luck that it did not work out. It could not work out because it was done for the wrong reasons. From Sheryl's point of view it had been a marriage of convenience, the convenience being the acquiring of status, that of being the wife of a Wall Street banker. From Harry's point of view he thought that he had been suckered.

They managed to stay together for almost three years. Deep down inside Harry was unhappy, which manifested itself in his lacklustre performance on the work front with frequent absentmindedness and an altogether unsatisfactory attitude towards his job. So when Black Friday came around, Harry was in the right place at the right time to push the wrong button. On the home front there had been a lingering crisis, which was gradually getting worse. When Harry got fired Sheryl had had enough. She simply threw him out of the house, called her lawyer and filed for divorce.

End of story.

I looked at Harry, who was somehow relieved when he had come to the final stage of his tragedy.

"So, now you know it all, old boy." He breathed a sigh of relief and leaned back.

"Harry, if you weren't a dying man I would hit you over the head for always calling me *old boy*. I'm not sure I like it." I wanted to change the subject, before Harry had time to start brooding again. It worked. He grinned.

"You're right. In the future I'll call you *old man*." We both laughed and for the first time since our arrival in the cabin Harry was no longer dying.

Then we both fell silent, each of us feeling a need for privacy and a chance to be alone.

Harry had got me thinking. His incredibly frank account of what must have been his most fundamental experience with the opposite sex had put me in a pensive mood.

Poor sod, old Harry, I thought.

How very different from mine his whole past and personal history had been! Everything was different between the two of us. Whilst Harry had spent practically all his life until leaving for college not only in the same town but in the very same house, surrounded by the very same people, parents, grandparents, neighbours, buddies, shopkeepers, in short everybody, my past had been characterised by constant, never ending change.

This was due, primarily, to my father's occupation which was as much of a mystery to me as it was to everybody else. He worked for the British Government in the Colonial Administration. The exact nature of his activity came under the terms of the Official Secrets Act, which to the British Civil Service must have carried more weight than the Bible. I remember one evening when we were sitting on the terrace of our house in Mombasa, facing the Indian Ocean; I had asked him what exactly it was that he did. With his eyes on the faraway horizon and without looking my way he said with sadness in his voice, "I am helping to undo the British Empire."

Not asking questions of this nature was almost law in our family and must have had its roots in how my parents had met. My father had been in the RAF in World War II and had soon found himself flying special missions into occupied France, mostly in an aircraft known as the Westland Lysander, a big, single-engine special missions aircraft, not all that much different from our now defunct Beaver. On one of his many missions he had to bring back a group of French *Résistance* activists, who were needed in England to help brief people that were to go into the field. This group had included a French woman who before the outbreak of the War had been attached in some undisclosed role to the British Consulate General in Marseille. She was strikingly beautiful, full of life and energy and soon to be my father's wife and, in due course, my mother.

When World War II was nearing the end in Europe my father stayed in the RAF and was immediately posted to East Africa. The government did not want to lose any time in stabilising the situation, as was then thought necessary. The numerous side effects of World War II had helped to kindle in the peoples native to Africa a desire to shake off foreign rule and the first ripples of the tide that was eventually to sweep across all of Africa, culminating in the various freedom movements, could be felt. In the midst of all this I was born, a British kid with international parents, in a country that was my home country by default rather than intention. I was a Colonial, as schoolmates in England would subsequently refer to me.

We lived in a small expat community in Mombasa along with the various other members of the Colonial Service that were going after first His and then Her Majesty's business in that particular part of the world. People came and went with changing duties and assignments, which meant that I had practically no steady school buddies. I was a bit like what in America came to be known as the service kids, who followed their parents around the globe from Mons to Tokyo, Honolulu, Guam, San Diego or Pensacola which, by the way, had been Collins' successive stations. That was perhaps one of the reasons why he and I hit it off so well. We shared the common fate of rootlessness and the lack of a birthplace with which we could identify unreservedly and to which we could go back and call *home*.

Whenever possible my father would take my mother and me along on his travels, which we both enjoyed immensely. I came to meet many of his colleagues and was impressed by the general standard of work ethics, personal integrity and dedication to duty that prevailed. And I was equally impressed by their capacity to consume incredible quantities of gin and tonic without seemingly getting drunk. As I concluded much later, it was their escape route from being denied the option of seeking sexual pleasures above and beyond what king and country allowed, foregoing the liberties that have become commonplace in our present time. In those days the finest and most capable and brilliant men appear to have opted for a career in HM's Colonial Service, dedicating their energies to building the British Empire, carried along by the fine spirits of *Messrs. Gordon, Walker, Whyte, Mackay et al.*

It is very hard for me to describe the relationship between my parents, in particular whether it was love, passion or whatever else that had brought and kept them together. The one thing I noticed about both of them was a deeply rooted sense of caring about each other, respect and gentleness in dealing with one another. Both my parents had been brought up with moderation in a Protestant environment and were not given to blind adherence to dogmas of any kind. They were not deeply religious, but agreed on certain fundamental principles for the conduct of one's life and had firm beliefs to guide them. That had given them great confidence and a generally positive outlook on life and the future. Once when my parents had an argument, which hardly ever happened, I could not help noticing that my father had simply abandoned his position, without even trying to put up a fight over it. I wasn't going to get involved but my father must have noticed that I had a question mark all over my face.

"Women play an important role: They are the bearers of new life, create life inside their bodies, men cannot. That's why they deserve our respect. It's not important to win an argument here and there. What's important is to acknowledge that there are greater things in life. Ultimately, a man finds happiness when he looks into the eyes of his woman, his happy woman. Why risk that for the sake of winning a little quarrel?"

Later in life I had to think about this event. It was decisive in defining my own attitude towards women. They were to be treated with respect, no matter what. This was to manifest itself, when things could so easily have gone the other way. So you might say I was very much a creature of my upbringing – and regardless of all else I am grateful for it, wouldn't want it any other way.

Education on a personal level for me meant elementary school in Mombasa with a number of other expat kids, followed by boarding school in England for my secondary education. Elementary school in Kenya was fun; boarding school in England was plain bloody awful. I thought that I was lacking in all the essential things that all the other boys had, an *English* family, a house in the country, and the right accent. At home it had not mattered. My mother spoke English with a distinct French accent, my father sounded undeniably Scottish and I had no particular accent at all. I could manage to put on a 'posh' English accent for about five minutes, if I tried very hard. But soon I would give myself away and become the laughing stock of all the other boys, so I stopped doing it.

The highlights of my adolescent life were the summer holidays, spent with my mother's relations in the South of France. Therefore it should not come as too much of a surprise that the few lasting friendships that I developed go back to these visits.

Then I met Louise. It was an instant feeling of closeness. Our favourite activity consisted of long walks in the forest, spent mostly holding hands, talking, listening and Louise smoking like a blast furnace. Smoking was an irritant for me because I simply did not like it. I objected to it for a number of reasons; health, common sense and some ridiculous, prudish concept of the 'immorality' of smoking. I criticised her smoking on every possible occasion, which she resented. This only changed when I discussed the subject – alas too late - with an older and wiser friend. He simply asked me whether I was happier without her and no smoke or with her around, tolerating that small irritant which, after all, was her business rather than mine.

We ran around together for three years, the summer vacations of three years. Whenever I had to go away I immediately started missing her immensely. I felt that deep surge of emotional pain that I had never experienced before.

My life changed suddenly when my mother died of a tropical disease and my father perished in a plane crash in Southern Rhodesia shortly thereafter while on an assignment for the government. For the time being this meant a sudden end in my life to any connection with Africa.

I had nobody to go back to, nor the freedom of choice if I had wanted to. Relatives on my father's side, who had immigrated to California, took me into their home. That is why I finished my secondary schooling by graduating from high school in California, which added a totally new perspective to my life and removed the last remaining traces of my British accent, for the time being.

I missed both my parents very much, although I had seen very little of them, with me being at boarding school or my father away on government business most of the time that I got to spend in Mombasa. It was the spirit that they had created and conveyed, the enchantment, the optimism and the unshaken belief that in the end all things would always turn out for the better. Therefore, I came to think of my childhood and youth as a very happy time of my life. It provided a good foundation for what lay ahead.

The senior high school year in California led to a college scholarship, which I was only too happy to take up for a bachelor's degree in aeronautical engineering. When I got back to Europe on vacation for the first time after two years' absence my first action was to go to Marseille to see Louise. We had been writing each other all the time, but the distance and my despair had not helped.

As soon as we came face to face again for the first time there followed a shock. Louise had not expected me for another week. I had cut short attending a seminar. She was in tears when she told me that she had accepted an invitation from someone I did not know, to accompany her to her high school graduation ball, the *baccalauréat* or *bachot*, the greatest event in a young French person's life. Overreacting I left the scene in anger. Ill advised words were uttered. I had nobody to talk to and did not possess the wisdom or maturity that I would have needed to handle this situation properly. I had a somewhat pompous notion that she had let me down and now had to come back to me.

She did not.

I felt drained and empty as these memories took possession of me. Saddened I had gone back to America. Without being consciously aware of it I must have changed into being a different person, I mean my attitude and outlook on life. The loss first of my parents, then my country of birth and residence and on top of all that the one person I really cared about were a bit much for a young lad to shoulder all by himself. But I had no choice; there was now nobody else in my life to whom I could run with my sorrows. At least so I thought.

I did not have the insight to reach out for Louise again. A deep underlying sadness was substituted for positive action. That is the truly sad part of the story. For whatever it's worth I would have nobody else to blame but myself. I retreated into my own fortress of solitude.

During the time that followed, reading books became a passion. Besides endless rows of Raymond Chandler and James Hadley Chase mysteries I remember two books that stood out from the rest. One was written by a young Chinese woman who was caught up in the upheaval of the Chinese revolution under the most dramatic of circumstances. She was a medical doctor, the child of an English father and a Chinese mother from Hong Kong. Her name was Carla Cheung. The events of the revolution had left Carla stranded alone in Shanghai. From there she crossed the country until finally settling down in the relative comfort of the then still British Crown Colony of Hong Kong, not without having had to make a few little detours via such remote places as Beijing and Kunming and most of it on foot. I immediately fell in love with her and found that much in the circumstances of her life related to my very own existence.

It may have been just a book to others but for me it became reality in the very vividly imagined, beautiful and sparkling personality of Carla Cheung, her determination, the will to prevail, her cheerfulness – no matter what – and an indestructible confidence that she was going to meet up with the one great love of her life, sooner or later.

With the invaluable benefit of hindsight the realisation started creeping up on me that this experience was not all that dissimilar to what happened between Harry and Hazel, except that theirs had been hands-on-physical, in a manner of speaking, at least eyes-on, whilst mine was emotional and spiritual and the mind produced the rest. When that notion hardened into something that I accepted as known fact I realised that I owed Harry a bit more respect than I had been showing towards him, time to start climbing off a rather high horse.

The other book from that period that stuck to my memory was by Kahil Gibran, a Lebanese author. Its title was *Broken Wings*, beautifully written and incredibly sad, describing the events in the life of a young woman that through a harsh and uncaring society around her was denied the fulfilment of her life's passion and her one and only love. Books as this one should have been banned, at least kept out of the reach of young potential heroes like me, for it laid the foundation in me for what I was later to identify as the 'Sir-Lancelot-Syndrome', which was to manifest itself in the subsequent phase of my life.

I completed my studies in America and returned to England, first to do my national service in the air force, the RAF. Because I had already acquired an engineering degree in aviation the RAF put me into ground support operations, never making even the slightest attempt to teach me how to fly. But they did teach me a whole lot of other things that over time were to come in handy on numerous occasions. Once they had had enough of me and let me go I went back to college in England for a master's degree in aeronautical engineering. My pilot training was to come much later.

As I thought about this my initial perception that Harry's life and mine had evolved in completely different ways was cast into doubt. Weren't there perhaps some quite significant similarities, a pattern of sorts? I had something to think about at any rate. It was becoming clear that Harry was not the only one who had to work out something that lay buried deep inside him.

I thought it was time for a break, to let the mind rest on something closer to our temporary home, like checking the weather and seeing whether Harry was still alive. But there was no need to worry. If anything, it was snowing even harder than before, Harry was now sound asleep and the chance that an aircraft would fly overhead looking for us and we would fail to notice it was absolutely zero under the present weather conditions.

Later Harry and I were sitting down for a meal, eating in silence, more corned beef and military rations. It tasted great and the tea was nectar. Harry had become much more relaxed. He smiled when he said to me,

"You know, I feel much better, having told you my story. It's like a big load has come off my chest, something that has been weighing me down all this time. I think I'm beginning to feel a new kind of freedom."

“Yeah, Harry, I understand fully what you’ve been going through.” In fact, far from my initial assessment, I had been coming to the conclusion that Harry had had a pretty good case. It was time to look at my own situation. Not that I wanted to tell him about it, but I had some figuring out to do.

“We can make life as complicated or straightforward as we like.” My optimism was perhaps a little bit ahead of my state of enlightenment when I said that, which was not lost on Harry.

“Up to a point.” Harry looked very thoughtful.

“Very true.” And with this profound statement from me the conversation ended, for the time being.

I did another weather check. When I opened the door, I managed to get about two feet away from it before the biting, cold wind drove me back into the relative warmth and shelter of the cabin. I was not missing anything out there, so I might as well enjoy myself and delve back into that rich world that I could only see when I closed my eyes.

The One-Shot-Mission

"What if you miss the approach . . . if you have to go around?"
"You don't, this is a one-shot-mission."

In some ways working in aviation can teach you things that you do not easily find elsewhere. This applies in particular to mistakes which are 'non-survivable', where you get killed if you screw up. It's as simple as that. Sometimes we run up against a situation where we have only one chance to get it right. It's got to be spot on. If it is not, we fail with disastrous consequences. This was brought home to me very early in my flying career, when I first set out to learn to fly. My teacher was a man named Dan, who was looking back on a career as an accomplished demonstrator and test pilot for one of the well-known manufacturers. When he became sick and tired of 'going by the book' he opted instead for a career as his own boss, dividing his time between bush-piloting, teaching people how to fly and ferrying small aircraft across the Atlantic to Europe or back. I have often been attracted to working with people like Dan who would just not fit behind an office desk. Being through with 'going by the book' can be taken literally with him. He was always good for the unusual and the unexpected. My first experience flying with him has to be filed under 'unusual', which set the tone for everything else that was to follow for as long as I was his student.

"Well, that's it for Reykjavik." Dan looked my way and gave me his pleasant, heart-warming broad grin. "They're closed on account of weather with no prospect of change over the next twelve hours. Our endurance is another nine. So Iceland's no-go." He had said it with that casual cheerfulness with which the headwaiter of a gourmet restaurant will tell you about the dinner options. There was no suggestion that we might crash into the sea, having run out of fuel, if we did not manage to find somewhere else on dry land to go to. We were above the big Atlantic, about halfway between Newfoundland and Iceland. I was sitting in the right-seat, the co-pilot's spot. Just sitting there was all I was contributing, because I was not yet a qualified pilot. Two days earlier Dan had come to me with that innocent look on his face:

"Could you pop down to the medic for a routine check-up?"

I did wonder why, but after a day's schooling to prepare for my first flight with him I was too tired to argue and simply went. As it transpired later, I passed a Class One Medical, which means I was fit to fly, in reality of course really more like fit to sit in the cockpit of an aircraft.

Dan had to ferry a small twin-engine aircraft across the Atlantic to England. It was certificated to be operated by two pilots. In real English that means it had an official certificate that said there had to be two of you to fly it legally, a pilot and his co. Dan did not want to take along a 'proper' co-pilot, partly because he thought he did not need one but also to save money. So in order to be legal, crossing the North Atlantic with a correct two-man cockpit crew he signed me on as a student pilot, a formally correct and legitimate move, as he was a licensed flight instructor. That was how I came to embark on what must have been one of the longest ever first training flights for a novice pilot with absolutely zero flying experience, from Gander, Newfoundland, to Shannon, Ireland and onwards to England.

The supreme law in aviation is 'things ain't what they seem to be' and after a picture book sunshine departure from Gander the weather was getting progressively worse, once we were out beyond the point of no return, out of range for a return to Gander for fuel or to land there and sit it out until the weather improved. So, here we were, flying on instruments, going nowhere, as far as I was concerned.

"Looks like the only option is Narsarsuaq." And then, as an afterthought, Dan added "Shit."

"No good?" I asked.

"No, no, just a little detour."

Narsarsuaq is an airport, more of a glorified landing strip in Greenland. Situated in a fjord, running in from the sea, it is quite famous in its own particular way among pilots who have landed there. I was soon to find out why. Even seasoned old dogs tend to refer to their first landing there as 'interesting' or 'unusual', both being outrageous understatements. For the next hour Dan was busy working out the new routing and getting Air Traffic Control organised over the radio.

After we had lumbered on in silence on the new heading for quite some time he said all of a sudden, "Well, we're about ten miles now, out of Narsarsuaq." After that Dan had become tense, the personification of high-carat concentration and professional dedication. When I tried to speak to him, he motioned me to be quiet. By the way things looked this was now far from a routine mission.

When for a brief moment he was a bit more relaxed, I asked him, "Is there anything that you know which I don't?"

He looked at me and gave me his warm, broad and confident grin. "I'll tell you, in a moment."

Up ahead there was now a bank of fog and I could not see a thing. Dan looked in my direction and shouted, "this is it. We're on short finals."

This surprised me yet again, for in addition to the fog that I could see ahead of us through the windshield I did not have the foggiest idea where we really were. During the next few moments the tension came through to me. Dan was now completely incommunicado and totally concentrated, watching his flight instruments and constantly making little, almost unnoticeable adjustments on the controls.

Without any warning first some open water and then a stretch of tarmac suddenly jumped up towards us out of the haze and fog. Within an instant we were on the ground, tearing along what looked like a pretty narrow runway. Dan had his feet on the brakes, reversing the pitch of the propellers and revving up the engines, to use the reverse thrust as an additional brake to slow down the aircraft.

As the speed dropped to taxiing I looked ahead through the windshield and was equally amazed and horrified. Ahead of you at the end of a runway you normally look at open landscape. Not here. There was a hill that looked to me like it was rising right out of the tarmac. There were more hills and even the side of a cliff next to the runway. I looked at Dan in total bewilderment.

“What if you miss the approach at Narsarsuaq, if you have to go around?”

“You don’t.” He looked at me and grinned. “This is a one-shot-mission.”

As the memory of this event came back I had to think of our choice of partner: For life. That is a one-shot mission, if there ever is one, at least for many of us. It certainly had been for me. The way I had handled my ‘one-shot-mission’ was the reason why I was now bush piloting in Alaska, sitting in a log cabin in the middle of nowhere instead of on my boat somewhere between Hawaii and Tahiti.

It had started with a picnic. Perhaps that was my first mistake, for it had put me completely at ease. Of course, that had been the reason for a picnic in the first place. Chris and I wanted to let off steam, celebrate our return to the world of the living. We were flat mates and had both just completed our studies and graduated to become Masters of Aeronautical Engineering. I had not contented myself with a mere Bachelor’s, acquired in California, but had returned to England for a Master’s. To mark the occasion with a worthy end to years of blood, sweat and tears a picnic in the New Forest would be exactly what was called for. So we put out the word among our friends and colleagues, trying to get together about a dozen couples to help us celebrate. Despite an initial enthusiastic reaction one after the other came up with an excuse. When the big day finally arrived, it was down to just Chris and myself and four girls: Ingrid, just in from Sweden, Jennifer, a liberal arts student from Birmingham, Julie from Paris with an undisclosed agenda and Lydia from Cairo, who was in London to receive the finishing touches to a ‘good education’.

After a brief discussion Chris and I decided to go on regardless. What the hell! We just wanted to have a nice day out in the open. The company of four attractive young women could not possibly stand in the way of that! It was a perfectly enjoyable day, with even the English weather on our side and not a cloud in the sky. Our attention was about evenly divided between lighting a small, very professional campfire and barbecuing a limitless supply of steaks and sausages, talking to the girls and otherwise doing nothing. As we were both driving - I had my car and Chris had insisted on coming along on his Vespa motor scooter - alcohol was not on the agenda, nor did we miss it, for we had only just emerged from a succession of extremely alcoholic 'victory celebrations' with our buddies. All good things have to end some time and so did this delightful day in the English countryside. After we had cleaned up the place, Chris and Ingrid suddenly vanished on the Vespa, leaving me with the task of taking the other three young beauties back to London and safely home. As it happened, Jennifer and Julie both lived at the same student hostel near Regents Park and were the first to get off, leaving me alone with Lydia for the final mile and a half to Finchley. This little journey was quite uneventful. I received a kiss on the cheek and a hug from each of the girls and drove back to my place in Hammersmith, a happy young man without a care in the world.

A few days later a young woman whom I did not know rang my doorbell and introduced herself as 'Lydia's best friend'. She conveyed her friend's greetings and best wishes, somewhat formally, and told me that Lydia had been taken ill and was, unfortunately, unable to come to the Foreign Students' Ball with me. I was puzzled, for I had already decided not to go and had no recollection of inviting anybody.

I definitely had not invited Lydia. Not that I would not have liked to. It simply hadn't occurred to me and, quite frankly, I didn't want to go. I was getting tired of all the partying and celebrating and was eagerly looking forward to the 'real life', whatever that would turn out to be. The friend also delivered a letter from Lydia, along with the verbal message. When she had gone I opened it.

'Dear Jack, Thank you for such a delightful day. It made me very happy.
Kindest regards,
Lydia.'

At the bottom was Lydia's address and telephone number. Although I had taken her home the other day I doubt very much whether I would have found the way to her front door again, even if I had wanted to. How thoughtful! In the letter there were also some pressed wild flowers. I was touched, not being used to this kind of attention. A bit nineteenth century, I thought, but nice.

Lydia

'To engage the good offices of logic and reason when dealing with a woman is like trying to nail a pudding to the wall.'
Ascribed to a European Elder Statesman

On the day of the Foreign Students' Ball I called her.

"I'm sorry you have been taken ill and cannot go to the ball."

"Oh no!" Her voice sounded surprisingly energetic, not at all as if she was looking a tragic and premature death in the eye. "I feel much better now! My friend brought me some medicine which really worked miracles!" As I hesitated a little, surprised, for this had been totally unexpected, she added "yes, I really feel fine. If you still want to go to the ball tonight it would be all right with me."

Snap!

A more experienced man would have heard the trap go shut!

That was the moment when everything started to happen in its mysteriously inescapable way. Up to that point, at the drop of the notorious hat, I could have hopped on the Hammersmith & City Line to Paddington, boarded the 10:24 for Cardiff and gone fishing for a week. Chances are I would not have remembered her or if I had, it would have been a thought like, 'what a perfectly civilised, fine young woman'. I would have recalled an enchanted day and the lovely company. Rare images of a sun-soaked New Forest would have given me heart-warming memories, something to feed on during rainy weeks to come. But she would not have haunted me in my sleep and I would have moved on in life without ever looking back.

I picked her up at about six o'clock that evening. She looked delightful, a bit formal, but graceful and very attractive. Women can do that kind of thing. After all, that is what Nature has equipped them with, the ability to be so outrageously attractive. The only thing I could do was to surrender to the magic.

Lydia fascinated me. That was one half of the equation. The other one was that I was alone, I was longing for a soul mate and I had been alone for much too long. At that time I did not think of the Foreign Students' Ball as the breakthrough in our relationship. This had a complex start. I wanted to run away yet felt strangely and mysteriously attracted to her.

I simply did not know what to do, how to deal with the situation, how to deal with Lydia. There were a few things that did not make it any easier. She grew on me, pulled me in and took a hold of me. In addition, there was the fascination of another culture and another world.

But even more than that there was the fascination of Lydia.

To anyone who met her one of the first impressions she conveyed was an aura of utmost integrity and sincerity, which adorned her like another woman would wear a fur coat. But for Lydia it was natural, like a second skin. Even if this may look like a chauvinist's attitude, the epitome of arrogance, judging someone by their human value and their quality such an attitude is the last thing that I have in mind if I speak of Lydia as a thoroughly good, valuable, solid person, a truly fine woman.

There was her graceful appearance, her pleasant and charming demeanour, her thoroughly civilised attitude and the way in which she went about life in the widest sense. Even someone who was not exactly a fan of hers would have conceded that Lydia was quite simply a person of great substance.

I was awed.

I was somehow overpowered.

I was completely overpowered!

Then there was the other side. I loved to dance; she would trip over her own feet, trying to fall in step with the rhythm. I loved music, any music. She liked to sing and whistle, but so badly out of tune that I experienced physical pains, listening to it. At first I was excited when she told me that she played the piano. But when she did I had to find some pretext to leave the room. Admittedly these were very superficial observations that only touched on a minor segment of her personality and would not do her justice.

I could think of at least one woman that I knew, a beautiful, young and by now quite famous singer, the virtual embodiment of all the wonderful things that I would associate with music, who apart from her undisputed art and talent was a perfect bitch. She was possessive and jealous to the point of deliberately starting a nuclear war, if given the chance. I met her just before she had her big breakthrough. We went out together briefly, until I just could not handle her any more and torn apart between attraction and sheer outrage put her on my ALP list, which stands for 'avoid like the plague'. Although delightful to listen to on the concert stage, she was totally unbearable in real life. That comparison, completely out of focus, idiotically narrow-minded and absolutely irrelevant, in some inexplicable and irreversible way started tipping the scales in favour of Lydia, slowly at first but the steadily followed – as happens so often.

There are so many sides and facets to someone's personality. I tried to deal with this rationally, to put the emphasis on the right things, the essentials, not the side issues, however annoying or tedious some of these may become if things go the wrong way. But the real point, the hard truth, was the fact, established with perfect twenty-twenty hindsight that I was not dealing with this as a lover, a man in love. We had not really bonded in a way that lovers do, with deep passion to the point of switching off one's senses, with total disregard for practical issues. I had embarked on the hopeless and ultimately futile attempt of making the right decision on the grounds of reason, logic and whatever else might come into play, whilst trying to ignore the magic powers of sexual and emotional attraction.

Dammit!

However, all logic and reason aside: The truth, the whole truth and nothing but the truth . . .

I desired her.

Sexual starvation must have come into the equation somewhere. Was it something more deeply rooted? I did not know. But the fact that I asked that question somehow also gave the answer. There was a lot that was there, but there was also a lot that was not.

I was getting myself deeper and deeper into emotional fudge. Without any compelling thrust from my feelings or conclusive evidence provided by the heart, be it for lack of insight and understanding or because it simply was not there, I found myself relying on the instruments with which I was only too well familiar: logic and reason. However, to use the words of a much revered, older friend: 'to engage the good offices of logic and reason when dealing with a woman is like trying to nail a pudding to the wall.'

The end result was that neither logic nor reason told me what to do. I simply did not know, was lost, all at sea with no shore in sight and had no one to turn to. So things started going the way, which they had to from this point onwards. It was already too late to run. Fate, my fate, had turned into a wild horse that was galloping up the notorious garden path.

We started going out together. Lunch, dinner, the cinema, walks in the park, walks down Regent Street, walks up Regent Street, sitting on the bank of the Thames watching the tide come up and watching the tide go down again. We talked, I about myself, what little came to the fore without the use of force and physical pressure, she about herself, her youth, her family, her past and previous life, her hopes, dreams and ambitions.

When she was ten years old her parents moved from Beirut, where she was born, to Cairo, where her father owned a very successful and substantial business. She referred to herself as a 'Christian Lebanese' or sometimes 'Lebanese Christian'. No matter which way she put it, the emphasis was on the 'Christian'. That mattered to her. In Beirut a large segment of the population was of the Christian faith and the culture and society that go with it. When you are surrounded by like-minded people, the things you have in common with them do not stand out. They are natural and receive little attention. Once they got to Cairo that changed. Although they encountered complete religious tolerance they were now in a Diaspora, an isolated outpost of Christianity and if your father is the very pillar of the church that will transmit itself into all facets of your daily life. Besides, her father made sure of that.

Apart from being the kingpin of the local church he was a real tycoon, a man who knew best what was good for his family and saw to it that they got it. The one thing he wanted his eldest daughter Lydia to find was a good husband. Hence she received an education that would open doors for her: The right doors. She was well prepared for the society in which they moved. Her father had a clear idea of whom he was looking for and what the perfect man had to be. And it was becoming obvious to me that that would not be me, more likely a government minister's son who some day would also be a government minister or himself a tycoon, someone of unquestionable credentials, impeccable family history, the right religion, culture and society. Do I need to go on? I could think of a long list of all the things I either did not have, not represent, not stand for or not believe in.

Swell!

So what was I doing, still running around with her? She was giving me a more than perfect excuse to bow out gracefully in a decent and perfectly acceptable way without hurting anybody's feelings. At least I thought so and should have jumped for joy, a free man again.

Instead of accepting the formidable and prohibitive circumstances as an excuse to cut and run I suddenly saw myself challenged, which made me intensify my efforts rather than running away. Fascination, sexual attraction and the will to master a man's noblest task in life combined in me to create resolve to succeed with vigour, valour and determination.

A woman had entered my life. I had not looked for her, had not hunted her down until the pattern was reversed. The thought of her apparent unavailability and the denial of presumed endless future happiness brought out the wolf in me, the up and coming top-dog. When challenged in his basic male instincts the somewhat fearsome male, who had shied away from captivity, turned around and rose to a vision that had crept into his state of mind to become his destiny.

In all this Lydia was by no means an innocent bystander. Much as I would like to show her as a true angel she hardly missed an opportunity to conjure up the spectre of her father's machinations to find her the right husband. She kept me in a sustained state of anxiety. She did absolutely nothing to dispel the notion that, if on her return to Cairo her father were to say, 'my daughter, meet your future husband,' she would answer, 'yes, father.'

Rational thinking tried to convince me that she would not do such a thing. Was I absolutely sure? No, I was not. She contributed her part to keeping me on edge. It would have been an understatement to say that I was caught up in an atmosphere of having been thrown into a competitive environment. It was an environment of impending mortal combat! I saw myself marching into the arena of a medieval Royal tournament, from which only the victor would walk or ride away alive to receive the hand of the princess. I was faced by crushing competition, albeit invisible, which made it much worse, for it allowed the mind to conjure up all sorts of scenarios that all seemed to lead to the same end result, the vague image of someone stepping out of the haze and mist, picking Lydia up in his arms and walking off the stage while looking at me over his shoulder with a mixture of triumph and contempt.

Very theatrical, I agree. But let us not forget, we are dealing here with an as yet very inexperienced young man, inexperienced in the ways of the world, women and life; in short a real greenhorn. If the presumed competition had been Joe Bloggs from next door I would have known how to deal with that, sizing up the man, formulating the appropriate strategy and driving home the successful attack. But this was shadow-boxing at its worst, amplified through a combination of ignorance of the facts, anxiety and insecurity. The total irony was, I am not at all sure that I would have seen the necessity for any fight, if it had not been for the suspected existence of competing other men.

Lydia was employing her woman's powers to the full. She wanted me and did all she could to further that goal and ambition. That seemed to include a good measure of feminine trickery, maybe not deliberately, by design and with cunning. It must have been intuitive. She did what her inner voice told her to do.

I was the last Westerner that crossed her path. She had already spent enough time in the West not to know and appreciate the difference between being the obedient wife of an absolute pasha, even if she were able to latch on to a more enlightened specimen, rather than a perfectly normal bloke from the West. Thus she did absolutely nothing to put my mind at ease and create that calm and relaxed atmosphere that is of such great value when you are faced with crucial, far-reaching decision making.

Seemingly out of the blue she announced that her time in Europe was up and that her mother would come in a few days to take her back to Cairo, not directly but doing a round-robin tour of some important cities, where she was to meet equally important people, including a fair number of eligible ones. At first I was crushed. Then my two alter egos, the ardent bachelor and the future topdog, were locked in combat as to the outcome. Should I let her go or hang on to her? Here was another opportunity beckoning, to extricate myself with honour, like in 'doing it for her own good'.

But I could have spared myself any thought of that. She did not want to argue and she did not give me any choice. As things stood, she was going back home as ordered. Whatever I wanted to accomplish with regards to her and any possible joint future for the two of us would depend on my actions. If I wanted her I would have to take the initiative. She was not going to meet me halfway. She was expecting me to take the plunge, jump off with both feet into the unknown and no escape hatch at the ready.

The next few days were torture for me. I was desperately searching for the right answer, whatever that was, but no amount of thinking and reasoning got me any closer to that goal. As time available got shorter, the scenario became more and more complex, less and less clear. I needed to think without the emotions, from the head.

When outside help was not forthcoming I resorted to the one approach that had always worked for me when I needed to clear my head and think straight. I went for a very long walk, crossed Hammersmith Bridge to Barnes, and walked up along the Right Bank of the Thames, following its many twists and turns all the way to Richmond, the best of five miles, two hours at a leisurely pace. The cool September air had the desired effect. The longer I walked, the better I felt. When I finally reached the *Swan and Crown* my outlook on life was returning to its long-time normal.

After two pints of *Worthington's Best*, I was beginning to be my good old self again. At last, I thought. Now I would know what to do. I needed a face-to-face with Lydia. I did not think of this as a showdown, more like some kind of 'think-tank'. As it was to turn out that idea was utterly ridiculous. You do not have 'think-tank sessions' with a woman on matters of the heart! That notion in itself was an absurdity, even more outrageous than expecting pigs to fly. But how was I to know then?

I thought the occasion called for something above and beyond the ordinary. I was going to create a memorable evening, make her feel good, put her mind at ease and tell her the truth, whatever that was, straight from the heart as it would come to me then and there: No plan, no rehearsed plot and with heartfelt honesty and dignity.

So I got concert tickets, chamber music, Mozart and his friends. We both enjoyed it. After that the only logical progression towards excellence was a visit to *Lucas's* for some superb seafood. I wanted to create a relaxed, harmonious and peaceable atmosphere. All indications were that I had succeeded. Lydia was in a perfectly good mood, thoroughly enjoying herself.

The moment was now.

"Are you glad to be going home?" My question was absolutely sincere, motivated by genuine concern.

"How can you say such a horrible thing?" She gave me a look of total surprise, startled, almost unable to speak, doing so only with great difficulty. "I thought you loved me?"

I had expected a lot of things, but this was just about the only reaction that I had not. I was instantly overcome by a great sense of shame, like a traitor who has just been found out. It immediately put me on the defensive. Suddenly I felt as if I had done something very low, something inexcusable.

Lydia had stopped eating her meringue, her favourite desert and put her napkin on the table.

"Tell me what is wrong!" she demanded, giving me a long, searching look, as if to discover whatever it was that was driving a wedge between us. "Have I done anything to offend you?"

"No, Lydia." All my logic and rationale were gone. They vanished at the first sign of distress. I did not know what to do, didn't have the remotest idea.

Then the tears started flowing.

"I should have known that you don't love me. You only wanted to play with me." She started to sob uncontrollably, inaccessible to words, no matter how gentle or caring.

"Lydia, of all the things that I may or may not have done the one thing I did not do was play with you!" I raised my voice somewhat, for I felt quite emphatic about this point. I had definitely not played with her feelings and emotions.

My mood - up to that point splendid - collapsed in an instant. The evening was suddenly over before it had been allowed to start properly and in the fashion in which it had been intended or perhaps masterminded, albeit inadvertently. Had I really not somehow steered things into this unfortunate human relations disaster?

"Lydia, I just wanted to know how you feel."

"Please, take me home. I know what you wanted to tell me."

Try as I might, the conversation, what little of it there had been, had broken down beyond any hope of resuscitation. There was nothing else to do but take her home.

We had stopped communicating.

This is perhaps the point where I made a mistake for which I could be held responsible. The truth that I should have seen immediately was that we had never really communicated. We had never established the kind of relationship where you sense or understand the other person's true feelings, a bonding of the minds to take us above and beyond the persuasive powers of desire. But at the time I did not see that. All I did was feel awful about having obviously hurt her feelings through my crude and tactless remark. So she said and I took her word for it, unchallenged. And I felt hurt that my sincere efforts went unrecognised.

The evening ground to a premature end. It became only too obvious to me that I did not possess the powers to turn it around. There were plenty of people that I could think of who could have done just that, made one suitable remark, some wisecrack, possibly with a broad, innocent grin, held her hand and wiped the subject under the table. But not I! Unfortunately, I never had that ease with words and the presence of mind to master such situations. Instead, I had to suffer the consequences: take her home, a formal 'good night' without so much as a hint of a smile, followed by 'my mother will be here in three days' time to take me back' as her closing statement, leaving me high and dry, feeling lonelier than ever before and plain bloody awful.

That night brought no relief. Sleep did not come until the small hours of the morning, leaving ample time for endless torture. I got up late, starting in a bad mood what I expected to turn into a bad day. It goes without saying that this became a self-fulfilling prophecy. What else could have come out of my dark, dejected mood? Endless hours were filled with meaningless activities as I pottered around the house without producing anything noteworthy to show for it.

At 5:00 p. m. sharp the doorbell rang, tearing me out of a most destructive daydream, bordering on sheer masochism. I was being marched to the gallows and Lydia was about to put the noose around my neck, 'gently but firmly', if there was such a thing. After all, 'she did not want to hurt me', she suggested, as her lovely hands gently pulled the noose tight.

"Happy birthday!" With a warm smile Lydia handed me a bunch of beautiful wildflowers, followed by a hug and a long and affectionate embrace and a kiss.

"I had completely forgotten about that," was all I could say, when I finally managed to recover from what is commonly referred to as a mild state of shock. "You know, there aren't really a lot of people who remind me of my birthday." I was just saying something for the sake of it, to overcome the awkward moment. As if by magic my dark mood was gone, blown away like cobwebs in a warm summer's breeze. At that moment all that I could think of was that I was happy to see Lydia, overjoyed that she had come back, for somehow my vivid imagination had started evoking a loss-of-sweetheart scenario, persuading myself that I would never see Lydia again.

All of last night's anguish and anxiety were forgotten. We were happy together like we had not been before. I showed her my flat, which she had seen only briefly once before, just after we first met, when I wanted to show her how I lived. She liked my books and my records, my two treasures that I would not want to miss for anything in the world.

"Do you want to go out for dinner, Lydia?" I was careful not to jump any decisions on her, giving her ample time to say what she wanted to do.

"Why don't we stay here? Cook something for me. You said you can cook, Jack. Prove it." She smiled at me and followed it up with another affectionate hug.

"Yeah, let's stay here. Sure, I can cook. The question is whether you can eat it."

We both laughed, and there was nothing to remind anyone of the drama that had happened only a day earlier, threatening to crush the tender blossom of love. Before we knew it the midnight hour had come and gone, but Lydia gave no indication that she wanted to leave, to return home to her flat. Careful not to upset her again, I just kept my mouth shut and continued to enjoy her presence. Then, much later, we were both overpowered by the need to sleep.

To this day I have difficulty in piecing together what actually happened during this rather crucial stage of the encounter. I am afraid the disappointing truth is: nothing. Somehow we both wound up in bed, my bed. Chris, my flat mate, had left to return to Sweden a few days before. Technically speaking, his bed was still there and available. But that option was never discussed. Lydia and I simply got our clothes off, slipped into bed and went to sleep, without much fuss and bother, as if we had been a seasoned married couple.

If this looks like a roundabout way of seducing her, nothing could have been further from the truth. I did not try, she did not resist and nothing noteworthy happened until wake-up time, the next morning. I had made a conscious decision, followed by a superhuman effort, to avoid any sexual involvement, as I was afraid that it would complicate things further.

During the night I woke up a few times, holding Lydia in my arms. I must have felt like a true defender of virtue. A real Sir Lancelot! I was honour-bound, unable to drive home the ultimate man's quest, as if Excalibur itself had been lying between the two of us as a solemn reminder of the nobility of spirit that was being called to the fore here.

For Lydia this was not an issue at all. She had delegated the concern and care for every aspect of her well being to me and put her total faith and trust in me, including whether or not I would eventually give in to sheer lust and desire and simply take her. That in turn gave me the full responsibility for whatever happened, raising my level of involvement beyond negotiable limits and my commitment to a total and irreversible one.

She had placed her honour in my trusted care. Everything was now up to me. When you look at this with the eyes of the young people of today, at the end of the twentieth, early twenty-first century, you would be forgiven for thinking of what a long forgotten, medieval age this guy was coming from. I wonder myself.

Lydia simply took possession of me, ending the argument and creating a basic set of facts. Now it was for me to sort things out and make a success of the whole affair. I cannot say that she had done this against my fierce resistance. That would be an untruth. There would have been plenty of time and opportunity for me to step away from it all. I was caught because I had allowed myself to be caught. I had manoeuvred myself into an inescapable situation and I was beginning to face the consequences. There would still be moments to reconsider, re-evaluate. But the powers that had got me that far in the first place continued to prevail.

Her mother came and put a brave face on the situation. She seemed to see Lydia's point of view, her hopes as well as her fears about going back to the old life, with which she herself was only too familiar, having been the obedient wife for as long as she cared to remember. But she also knew that her husband would not accept me for all the many good reasons and selection criteria that he himself had put forward.

I showed the two women around London's normal tourists' sites as well as a few only known to the Londoner, which they both liked. Then they flew to Paris. I had started a job, which kept me in London during the week. But I followed them that weekend, to give them the insider's Paris, the whole shooting match: *La Tour d'Argent*, *Le Pied de Cochon,* and many more and less well known sites. My being not only a fluent French speaker but knowing the ropes around the French earned me a few brownie points, unexpected ones from mother and additional ones from Lydia, who noted it all with a great sense of pride and satisfaction. Her man managed all right out in the big, wide world.

While I returned to London for another week's work the two women gradually made their way to Brussels, where I joined them again for the following weekend. Both Lydia and I had become apprehensive and somewhat on edge. Suddenly our last moments together were there, before she had to go away and face whatever it was that her father had lined up for her.

Between the two of us nothing had been decided or arranged. There was no plan, no clearly defined program of any kind. I had not even proposed to her, so that she would not have been able to accept or reject my proposal. But that did not matter to her. Several times when I tried to get her to sit down with me to talk about things she did all she could to avoid just that.

Whether she did this deliberately or whether it just happened, we never did sit down together to talk things through. The moment came to take them to Zaventem Airport. Suddenly the last good-bye was there and gone again and I stood on the visitors' terrace, watching the Boeing 727 streaking into the sky over Brussels, bound for Rome. I did not take my eyes off it until it was no more than a tiny dot in a great big, blue and otherwise empty autumn sky.

It was a beautiful, sunny mid October Sunday afternoon. But I was blind to the magnificent Indian summer, which under normal circumstances would have overjoyed me. I was gripped by a deep sense of sadness. That did not change much as I drove back to the coast to take the ferry from Calais to Dover. I spent the whole journey on the afterdeck of the ferry, lost in thought, my eyes on the horizon. By the time the cliffs of Dover appeared on the star-board bow from out of the early evening haze I had restructured myself, sorted myself out to whatever extent you can sort yourself out if you are the born analytical thinker and have absolutely nothing on which to base any concept, plan or hope, but only a feeling of loss and sadness.

Lydia's desperately awaited first letter, the only one for a long time to come, was written in Beirut and reached me after she had got back to Cairo, arriving an eternity after her departure. They had gone first to Rome, from there to Geneva, then Zurich, Athens, and finally Beirut, before going back to Cairo. At each stopover they were immediately taken into the fold of some business friends of Lydia's father, who would take care of everything, including the as it seemed notorious party and reception which usually served to parade in front of her more and more candidates. I got the distinct impression that the whole expedition had been organised by her father as some kind of public relations tour, announcing the availability of his eldest daughter, 'showing the goods' and challenging the truly and I do mean truly eligible ones to step forward and throw their hat into the ring. The notion of the mediaeval tournament had not really been that far-fetched and was vigorously revived when I absorbed the contents of her letter.

Apart from informing me about all the horrible things that I just mentioned she wrote me that she really missed me and was very, very sad. Meanwhile I had sent a string of letters off to her home address without eliciting any response. Then finally, after three more desperately long weeks I got a second letter from Lydia, telling me that her father had intercepted my letters sent to her home address, without showing them to her. He did not approve of her ever seeing me or speaking to me again and she was, of course, not to write to me. The fact that she had done just that implied to me that she was not accepting her father's decree. Instead, she gave me an address c/o a friend of hers, so that we could keep in touch.

If I had been in any doubt about her father's feelings or intentions with regards to myself I had only to wait another day to get it from the horse's mouth. I was abruptly pulled out of the shower by the doorbell early the next morning, even before getting ready to leave for work.

"Telegram for you, mate - want to sign here? – thanks - cheers, mate - take care."

To this day I have no recollection of ever having received any good news by telegram. This one was not to be an exception. It was from her father; short, to the point and absolutely unambiguous:

Thank you for your interest in my daughter Lydia. In keeping with our long honoured family tradition I have made a decision about Lydia's future husband and my successor.

May God bless you.

Signed . . .

Of the many ways of saying 'no' this was perhaps the most definitive one, without ever even using the word itself.

I was crushed. I was devastated.

But then I was outraged. His last words in particular saw to that. In fairness to him I have to admit that in no way did he intimate that Lydia had agreed to anything. Good as that might have been it also signalled to me that she now only had me to get her out of this presumed impending personal catastrophe of being denied the freedom of choice and to be forced into a marriage that she did not want.

I admit that after Lydia's departure for Rome doubts had started gnawing away at my resolve as to what really was good for her and what was the best thing to do, all things considered. With his probably absolutely honest but equally ill-advised telegram her father had made the one big, final and irreversible mistake, if he had really wanted to stop me from marrying his daughter: He had challenged Sir Lancelot! Up to that point I might have caved in at any time, giving way to an emotional pressure that I could not handle any more. But this cable had to be the straw that broke the camel's back!

The chips were down.

I set to work on a D-Day scenario. I would go and get her out of there, come what may. I had stopped trying to figure out whether I was doing the right thing for the wrong reasons or the wrong thing for the right reasons or simply the right or the wrong thing for no matter what reasons. It did not matter any more. I would simply go and do it. I would get her out of there.

The chips were down indeed!

From here on, believe it or not, things became a lot easier for me. Not that the prospect of going into a foreign country to bring back a bride against the express wishes of her father was an easy and appealing one. What made things easier was the fact that I was now dealing with a project, something that could be planned and executed with foresight, diligence and in a responsible manner. Thereby the affair had moved into a terrain with which the analytical thinker and engineer was well familiar.

A plan emerged, Plan A, First Draft: go there, don't tell anybody, get her, bring her back, element of surprise, minimum risk of premature exposure and failure.

I thought about it.

Bad plan! It would not work for one simple reason: the human factor, Lydia. She would insist that I made at least one sincere and determined effort to convince her father, so that he would accept me and allow her to seek her personal happiness without hurting her parents.

Yeah, that is what it would have to be. So I came up with Plan B, which really was not a plan at all: Go there, request to see her father, ask for her hand in marriage and his blessing, obtain that and take her back. No element of surprise and not failsafe.

And if he continued to say 'no'?

Well, I would have to cross that bridge when we got there. There was no point in working myself into a frenzy trying to anticipate all the things that could go wrong. But if all else failed there would have to be a Plan C.

The first thing that came to mind was that I needed two commodities as a prerequisite to success: time to set my expedition up properly and money, working cash, to cover the various stages of the operation. By now it was early December, going on Christmas. Next Easter looked like a good date to shoot for. That would give me a few months for whatever preparations I thought would be necessary. And I set about doing everything humanly possible to boost my income situation: overtime, freelancing and volunteering for special assignments, the kind that included travel to a far away place, long hours and the potential for a success fee.

I can keep the next bits of the story short. Let us just look at the result. I did go to Cairo to face her father and her family. They were nice people, honest, law-abiding and righteous. At first dad seemed to like me, but things turned bad when his best friend was called in, to 'look me over'. Apparently he came out vigorously against me for a string of reasons that would fill the next two pages.

After about a week into my mission to Cairo – I had prepared myself and budgeted for up to four weeks – I was called into a family council, where dad once more thanked me, but said that 'as at that moment letting me marry his daughter did not seem like a good idea', given the fact that I was just starting on a career of which nobody seemed to know just exactly which way I was heading. Why didn't we give it, say, two years, for things to fall into place?

Let's face it, his position was not an unreasonable one, all things considered, that is if you try to see things from his end. I neither agreed nor disagreed but asked for time to think it over, which he said would be the proper thing to do. No doubt, I would come to the right conclusion, the one that would be best for Lydia.

"What happens to Lydia during the two years? Will you continue to try to marry her off to someone of your choice?"

"Of course, young man." He smiled at me, not at all an unpleasant smile. He was a man of the world, someone who commanded respect in a natural way and I could see nothing wrong with what he was doing, from his point of view. But that was not mine and not Lydia's, the way I saw it.

"Consider life a test. If you are meant for each other it will work out that way. If not, that's life."

As this was as far as he was prepared to go, I thanked him and made my exit. I had managed to pull Lydia aside earlier to agree a meeting point for next morning, when we would consider the situation.

"What do we do, Lydia?"

"You decide, Jack."

"Will you come back to England with me, when I leave?"

"Yes."

This had not been as easy for her as it seems. She loved and respected her father. The thought of going against his word must have been tantamount to the most horrendous sacrilege to her. Obviously, she had gone through her share of worries and anxiety.

Lydia had prepared nothing. She had given back her passport on her return to Cairo and was now without one. She had started working as a secretary, but her pay went to her father for 'safe keeping'.

This is not a travelogue about visiting the land of the Nile and the Pyramids. I want to limit this part of the story to what is really essential to understand the situation between Lydia and myself. The point is that we got it all together in a little over a week. Lydia deserves full credit for doing all that was in her might to move things along. Thus, on a Sunday afternoon – secretly and without having told anybody – we boarded a flight for London, ironically while her parents were attending a wedding, which they had helped arrange as go-betweens. That time-honoured custom still prevailed in these circles. For Lydia this was a stark reminder of what she was running from.

Getting away from Cairo and making it to London, safe and sound, without outside interference, was one thing, having arrived there quite another. It was a big anti-climax. Slowly we started to unwind and settle into a new normality of life. Then an envoy arrived from Cairo. It was her father's friend, the one who did not like me. He was supposed to persuade Lydia to go back. Lydia insisted that we extended the customary courtesies to him, met with him and listened to what he had to say. Later, when we were alone again in my bachelor's flat, which had now become our first home, I wanted to find out whether Lydia was in any way regretting our actions.

"Are you happy with what we've done, Lydia? Do you want to talk about it?"

She gave me a look of utter surprise, which then became a pained amalgamation of horror and dismay.

"You cannot mean that!" Outrage now joined the horror and dismay. "What is the matter with you, Jack? I do not understand your question. I agreed to come with you and here I am. What is there to discuss?" Then without any warning she started to sob. The tears kept coming, as if to wash away all the tension and anxiety of the period that lay behind us which for her, looking at her previously ordered life, must have been an upheaval, a total departure from the clearly structured, predictable way in which her private affairs had been run.

I held her in my arms until sleep finally came to restore her peace, at least outwardly. For the first time I had a premonition that we were wide apart on some fundamental issues, including one that was so very close to what I thought made up my personality, the way I functioned and was moving through life. At that time it was just a first inkling, a notion. The full weight of what I was to realise, in due course, had not yet hit me, but if it had it might have crushed me then and there. Lydia had grown up as the child of a benevolent tyrant. Of all the fathers that know best hers was the superlative, the one who knew it all. She had not been taught or trained to go through a decision making process. Whenever a decision had to be made, dad was the one who made it. Things were not discussed. He would do whatever it was that he did to arrive at a decision. Once he had done so, he would announce, no, pronounce it and that was it. There would be no discussion, let alone criticism, which was unheard of. Once the word was out, that was what one did.

It stood, forever, like a confession that you might make in an English courtroom, when the director of public prosecution had driven you into a corner: Once spoken it could never be retrieved or withdrawn. If you let slip a remark that you might have put your elbow in the victim's ribs on the long down-escalator at Piccadilly Circus, whereupon the latter fell to his unfortunate death, that was it, for the rest of your life, even if afterwards fifteen credible witnesses saw you play cricket at an international invitation tournament in Rio de Janeiro on the very same day, so that you could not possibly have done it. Your confession, spoken in an English courtroom, in despair, just to have peace, to be left alone, would take precedence over any other evidence. A man's word, once spoken, was irretrievable.

Forever.

That is how she expected things to be between the two of us! Lydia had formed her perception of a man after what she had come to know and appreciate about her father, who henceforth would provide the yardstick against which all other men were measured.

I do not know whether it was the foreign heritage in me, the continental streak, that made me look upon life as a long journey, along a path whose route and destination you did not know in advance. To me everything in life was open-ended, nothing to be taken for granted. Life for me was a challenge, a quest which, as you went along, might have to be reviewed as your enlightenment and awareness heightened and put you into the position to expand your aspirations.

In what concerned my outlook on life on a personal level, my soul mate, chosen by mutual consent, was to be someone with whom I could share my feelings and emotions as well as my concerns and anxieties, drawing strength and reassurance from arriving at beliefs and convictions that both could share. Lydia lacked any understanding of such thoughts, no matter how gently I put them to her. A word was a word. Once it was out, that was it, that was the decision and there was no need to talk about it. She had asked me for a decision. When I had made it she had accepted it and followed me.

There was nothing left to discuss! Not ever again.

I realised that from now on I was responsible for Lydia. She had placed that responsibility in my hands and she was depending on me to come true. For her there was no process of analysis and discussion, weighing arguments, until you both agreed on a common approach. She expected me to make the decisions, the right decisions.

There was nothing else to do other than to get on with it. So we set the date for the wedding, the sooner the better, I thought. As it turned out, I was eventually going to marry her without ever having proposed to her. No proposal had ever been accepted by her. We just simply did it. On the way to the registrar's office I turned religious. I prayed. I prayed that lightning would strike, the legendary bolt from the blue, and wipe me out.

Alas, my prayers went unanswered.

Home

An estate agent once tried to sell me a 'beautiful home'. When I suggested 'beautiful house' instead she stubbornly refused to acknowledge that there is a distinct difference.

"So, you were going home?" Harry looked at me expectantly. I think he had been getting bored, being left to his own devices. He wanted company. "Where is home anyway? You've mentioned Kenya, London, California . . . anywhere else?"

"It's not as simple as that. I have been wondering about that myself. How do you define home? What is it that earns a place that designation?" Harry had touched on something that had been troubling me for some time, not just recently. "Maybe it's easier for me if you tell me about yours, the place or whatever it is that you call home."

"A few years ago that would have been Peoria, Illinois, where I was born, where my parents live, where I went to school and where most of my friends and buddies are. For many people home is the place to which you return regularly on special occasions like Thanksgiving or Christmas. Don't you have the same?"

"Yes, in principle, although in the UK Thanksgiving is not as big a deal as in America. Christmas certainly is the one grand occasion. But you're saying that it's not quite as easy any more for you to say where home is . . . ."

"Yeah, that's right. The last time that I really thought of my parents' house as home was that fateful occasion when I got back from New York a happy bachelor and returned there a married man a few days later. After that everything changed. We got the condominium in Queens, I commuted to Manhattan for work and Sheryl was the happy mother of Karen and Peter for as long as it lasted and until I got chucked out." That memory still hurt; I could tell from the expression on Harry's face.

"You had a happy family, an attractive and beautiful wife and two attractive and beautiful kids. So that was home all right, wasn't it?"

"Don't be cynical, Jack, you already know the outcome of that story. It was home for the duration of my married life and when it stopped being that I became a man without a home, without home, a man with nowhere to go."

"I would guess your parents' place slipped back into pole position?"

"Not really, I'm sure you know what it's like. Once you've moved out and got married it's never like before, I'm sure it was the same with you, wasn't it?"

"Not really. You see, I lost my home just as I was turning seventeen, when my parents died and I had to leave Kenya, my country of birth, and go to California to live with relatives. I had a place to stay all right, but I never came to regard that as home. It lacked the one vital ingredient: sharing the place with your closest relatives like mother and father. My uncle and aunt were fine people but at that age a kid doesn't bond any more in the same way as one would with parents or a chosen soul mate. I had a comfortable and very much cared for place to stay, but something was lacking, something I cannot define or put my finger on.

When I married Lydia I thought we would raise a family in a happy home. But the way things developed we never grew into a real family. As she became increasingly disappointed with me, Lydia reverted to being her father's daughter. Emotionally and mentally she remained in his family, relied on that as her home and denied both me and the kids that which really makes a home, the love of a family. Lydia was a faithful, loyal and obedient servant. We never got any closer than that."

"Wow!" Harry was speechless.

"I've been thinking about this question a lot. Over time I have come to my understanding of what 'home' means to me. There is hardly another word that is so deeply steeped in emotions as the word home. It may mean different things to different people but there is one underlying quality that outshines every other: home is the place of the soul, where it finds warmth, comfort, shelter and protection when all else conspires against us and we are driven to the brink of despair. Home is where we long to be when there is nowhere else to go but above all it is the place where we hope to find peace. The more this is out of reach the stronger is our desire to go home. There are many people who have no home, due to any number of reasons: Floods, famine, acts of war or civil unrest and events that change maps. Home is unique - there's nothing like it."

"That hits the nail on the head; it's what we are all looking for when we think of home when all goes well," Harry looked thoughtful, "but it is a very idealistic view that doesn't match the everyday reality of people like you and me."

"Up to a point I'll go along with that. In America you've got language-confusion on top of all else. An estate agent once tried to sell me a 'beautiful home'. When I suggested 'beautiful house' instead she stubbornly refused to acknowledge that there is a distinct difference. But there is. You cannot sell the place of the soul, the home, just the bricks and mortar, as we say in England – I guess in America it's more like the two-by-fours and the plaster-board, the material shell. To make it into a home it needs a family to fill it with life."

"Yeah, that's what I was trying to say." Harry nodded his approval. "So, I guess we're both homeless, are we?"

"Sometimes it's hard to face certain uncomfortable facts, but when you look for the bottom line that's probably it. No family, no home, that's the sad truth. We've each got an ex-wife and two kids, so where do you figure with regards to yours?" I asked Harry.

"I've tried to maintain an amicable relationship with Sheryl. I see the kids from time to time and they enjoy that as much as I. Sheryl on the other hand never misses an opportunity to shower me with contempt and disapproval. That's a bit sad." This really was getting to him and in a sense it was affecting both of us. We were confronted with one of our great failings in life.

"So tell me, what exactly was or is it that you were so eagerly flying home to?" I could feel Harry's sincere interest.

"Hope. I guess it's hope more than anything else, the hope that at the other end of my journey I'll find what I've been longing for all these years, a place for my soul."

"Sometimes I think you only find that when you're dead, Jack."

"That's what the cynics say. You are still much too young for such a dark outlook, Harry. You have all opportunities ahead of you."

"So, what's your scenario, the wife, eh, ex-wife and kids?"

"Keith and Kathleen are both going to college. We've kept in close contact as much as possible. I've been treating Lydia with respect all along; she's their mother, I owe it to them and Lydia is reciprocating in the same way. Since our divorce there has never been an unfriendly word between us – she got married again and seems to be happy, which was a big worry off my chest when it happened."

"Her home is your kids' home, right?"

"Yeah, that's so."

"And not yours. That brings me back to my earlier question: What is it that drives a mature, balanced man-of-the-world like you to go looking for home when he knows as fact that his uncle and aunt in California are no longer there, his ex-wife and kids live in the house of another man and there isn't a living soul in Kenya that even remembers his name? Tell me, Jack, what is it?"

"It's hope, Harry, and longing. It's the deeply rooted desire to find it. The thought of home is what we treasure in our hearts and from which derives our strength to persevere when there is little else left. I shall be going home for as long as I live."

"So, back to my question: Where is that, Jack?"

"If I have to answer you right now I have to say that I honestly don't know."

Frustration

Day 5
And if nobody is tuned to your frequency that means nobody is receiving your signal, and your voice is never heard.
. . . time to shut down the brain and stop thinking.

Did I say the weather could not get any worse? Well, it did. Only one out of our five days in the wild had had weather suitable for visual flying operations. This was getting on our nerves. It was depressing and extremely frustrating for action people like pilots, who earn their keep by moving around. Much as we both would have liked to look upon this as some kind of relaxation and rest period, what kept us from doing this was the fact that we had absolutely no control over our situation. All we could do was survive.

At first I had a lot of recriminations about the loss of the aircraft, although there was probably precious little that I could have done to avoid it. But the longer I thought about it, the clearer it became to me that, as far as the company was concerned, we were looking at a cash sale of the old Beaver, as macabre as that may sound. Still, no pilot likes to walk away from a smouldering wreck. It gnaws at your professional pride. Admittedly, we had got a pretty good deal, all things considered. But if I had seen any reason for doing something, I would have gone and done it, if it had made any sense at all.

No matter what! That's how bad we felt.

Somebody! Come get us out of here!

But situations like this also contain a challenge. I do not like to be stuck with something that is suddenly sprung upon me and I am not very well known for accepting defeat. Things that go wrong do upset me at the moment of impact, when they hit me and it starts looking bad. But that is also the time when my mind begins to race, exploring every possible avenue, rescue, escape or whatever is called for. It was time to work on an active survival strategy, something a bit more dynamic than just sitting there waiting. It was time to make a plan.

It is essential to make a plan. It may, at first, not be the right plan. It is the fact that you start working on a plan that is so important, that you activate the resources of your conscious and subconscious personalities. There is no such thing as a wrong plan. The initial plan may be inadequate but plans can always be changed, updated, upgraded, expanded or modified. If you have no plan to begin with, there is nothing to modify, nothing that can be improved and thereby lead to your salvation. In short: no plan - no rescue, save for by *force majeure*, an-act-of-God, a miracle or the boys from base who against all odds and wrong location data for starters manage to find you before you starve or freeze to death.

By making a plan you make the one essential contribution to the continuation of your physical existence and that of the species: In order to extricate yourself from your predicament you exercise your willpower to survive, you hang on. Thus for me the important thing is to start work on a plan. Once I have that the problem turns into a project and the crisis is then handled professionally like any other task that has to be mastered.

I went through the options.

The crystal transmitter in its crude simplicity opened up a perspective, no matter how limited or unlikely. Some kind person had had the vision and foresight to leave it on a shelf in the cabin or simply had just forgotten it. I had tinkered with it. Obsolete in its technology or not, it was still a very basic and simple transmitting device. Our little disaster was turning into a survivable mission. My first plan was ridiculously simple:

Fix the transmitter!
Get it to work!
Raise base!
Give them our position
and wait for them to come and get us!

Child's play. But first I had to get it to work.

The principle of the fixed frequency crystal transmitter is simple: The crystal emits a constant frequency radio signal, oscillating on a particular wave-length, which is determined by the characteristics of your crystal. They surfaced in the 1920s to 1930s and were then briefly used by the military as location finders or homing devices. But technological development marched on so fast that they soon became obsolete and were forgotten. A small number from military surplus stock lived on to serve as locators for various things and as toys for enterprising school boys. Their drawback was the question of an adequate electric power supply so that you could create a signal and get it into the airwaves. At the time lithium and nickel-cadmium batteries were just being invented and unaffordable, limiting the use of the device to where you would find an adequate fixed source power supply or create the necessary power with the help of a dynamo. But let's not get too technical. Suffice it to know that all you've got to do is modulate a superimposed alternating frequency on the crystal's constant signal and you can transmit.

Basic!

Last night I had rigged an aerial, cannibalising one of the coil-spring mattresses, undoing some of the coils and connecting individual bits and pieces to make an adequate length of wire, suspended from the cabin ceiling and attached to the transmitter as its antenna. Similarly, I ran another end as the earth-link, connected to a spoon stuck into a crack in the floor. My improvised Morse key consisted of more bits of wire, closing the contact between power source and transmitter to get a signal into the air.

My electric power supply came from the batteries in the flashlight that I found in the Flight-Safety-Kit, still sitting next to the stove where I had set it down on our arrival in the cabin and then forgotten. When finally opening and inspecting it I found the flashlight. In addition there were a first aid kit, a hand-held compass, a two-day high protein ration pack and a Very or signal pistol with nine cartridges: red, white and green, three of each.

As for my radio signal the best I would be able to create would be a crackle, maybe just a little better than the normal static, because the voltage of my power source was low - no more than better than nothing.

'. . . da-di-da-di-da - da-da-da-da - di-da-da-di . . .' the company's recognition signal. I could not receive any signal nor did I have any way of telling whether anybody was picking up mine. This process needed a recognisable order. Therefore I transmitted to an improvised plan, which was based on our *Company Operations Manual* for restoring lost communications with base. During three consecutive hours you communicated for about three minutes on the hour, starting as precisely as you could on the 'zero' second. Once I had restored the transmitter to operational status I commenced when the next full hour came up until it was time to call it a day. I had no way of knowing whether I was getting through to anybody with my amateurish attempts at broadcasting.

Against all hope it had been another day of bad weather. Up to now there had been only one day with good flying conditions. Now it was low clouds and snowfall again. You would not put your dog out on such a night. I had to think of how the wolves were doing. The thought that they were out there was reassuring.

After setting up the radio I felt dejected and drained of energy. I did not have much hope that our transmitter would serve any purpose, it was just too primitive. For the first time since having become stranded in the wilderness I was feeling low, depressed, devoid of expectations of any kind. I was in a destructive mood. If Harry had said one wrong word, maybe I would have strangled him. The strangest thoughts started flashing through my mind. I was beginning to think incoherently. I had a feeling that due to some unknown force I was gradually going around the bend. It was time to shut down the brain and stop thinking. I had reached the moment when the availability of a bottle of *Famous Grouse* would have calmed the rivers of my mind enormously. The note of frustration that had been creeping into my system took hold of all of me, body, mind and soul.

I was ready to sign a pact with the devil. My mood had reached rock bottom and I could feel a streak of emotional vandalism coming on. If we had been on an expedition of some kind this would have been the moment for the team psychiatrist to step in and administer a sedative, before I started strangling poor Harry. Some basic instincts were taking over, laying bare the subconscious pattern of the mind of a creature in the wild that was about to fight for survival, if only for a fleeting moment, until a more rational side gained the upper hand once more.

Story-Telling Time

"This is skipper Uhuru to rescue helicopter, we're here to help, over."

Harry's mood improved surprisingly fast, I would say at about the same speed with which I was now driving myself into a state of despair. So I was glad that he broke our otherwise endless silence at the right moment to stop me from delving into yet another one of my closed-eye sessions in search of the ultimate truth.

"You really take this sitting around and waiting rather well, old boy."

"On the contrary, Harry." He had caught me off guard but I was grateful to him for taking the initiative. I can manage perfectly well on my own emotionally, but sometimes a friendly chat does help. This was one of those moments. "I'm not good at waiting for things to happen. I usually prefer to be involved in doing something that makes sense rather than sitting around. The mind can overflow with memories if you have too much time to think. Old stories suddenly come back, things you've seen or done."

"Yeah, Jack, by the looks of it you are the born thinker." Harry said it with a friendly smile. I thought that he was coping very well with the situation as time went on. Whatever had weighed him down had vanished and Harry was on the way up, more so than I was.

"Harry, have you ever had a situation that a certain story keeps popping up? I mean a specific event – and you go through it in your mind, again and again."

Harry sat up, attentive, eager to listen to what might come from me. "So you've got a story? Is it something that I would be allowed to hear?" He said it jokingly and smiled.

"There is something that bugs me, something that is missing in this little episode and I turn it over in my head again and again."

"Well, you've done enough turning-it-over-and-over in private. Let's have it out in public. I suspect it's entertaining?"

"It's one of my sailing adventures. The memories of it keep popping up – it happened this fall – just two months ago, so the events are still fresh."

"You're a sailing man? Where did this thing happen?"

"In the Irish Sea."

"Wow, of all places! That sounds really exciting! I grew up right in the middle of America. There is water in all four directions, the Pacific and Atlantic Oceans to the west and east and the Great Lakes and the Gulf of Mexico to the north and south, but all of them too far away to make a sailor out of me. But I always wanted to go sailing."

"You're still young enough to develop a few new pastimes, although with the sea it helps if you grow up close to it so that its character and spirit can grow on you. It's not really something you can learn in a day or two but maybe it's not too late and the mariner in you may still come out."

Harry had to laugh at the suggestion and then he wanted me to get on with my story. "You have a boat of your own?" he asked.

"Yes, many years ago I bought a share in a seventy-five foot trawler yacht, one of-them-going-round-the-world-type boats, really classy. Meanwhile I've paid out the other two part owners and have been renting her out to a charter company for the high seasons in the Mediterranean during the summer and the Caribbean in winter. One more charter and she'll be all paid up and clear. She's actually in the Caribbean this winter and after that she'll be all mine. That's when I want to pack it in at the company and turn my undivided attention to seafaring."

"You lucky sonofabitch," Harry made himself comfortable. "Tell me what happened."

"All right, here we go." I was pleased about the idea and began my story.

"It was last fall, at the end of the summer season in the Mediterranean. We had to take my boat from Barcelona to Dublin and put her into a shipyard for repairs and a general overhaul. I had managed to get away from work for four weeks. On such trips I sail with a crew of two, Paul, an ex-Royal Navy commander and keen yachtsman in his own right and Trevor, who is a professional yacht-charter crew member and a wizard with everything electrical and mechanical."

"Sounds like a fine team." Harry was listening attentively and enjoying himself.

"People I trust blind – with my life if necessary. We've been on many excellent trips together and know each other really well." I paused to have some of the tea that Harry had put in front of me and then went on with my story.

"We flew to Barcelona to take her over from the charter company and set out on the trip to Dublin, sailed through the Straits of Gibraltar, up the Atlantic Ocean, past the Bay of Biscay and into the Irish Sea. All un-eventful, routine, I'd say. My boat is called *Uhuru*, which is Swahili for freedom.

It was a bleak morning in early October with westerly winds, about Force 7 Beaufort, reaching gale-force at times and whipping up an uncomfortably high, choppy cross-sea with the occasional rogue or even mini-monster waves in between. The weather was chilly and very wet from all sides, spray and intermittent cold, driving rain. Things started happening at 10:20 GMT. I remember the time because at 10:00 GMT I had handed the con over to Paul and was now relaxing on the flying bridge behind the wheelhouse, admiring the beautiful, dark and mysterious fury of the elements.

Our position was about halfway on a line from Fishguard in Wales, UK, to Dublin, Ireland, tacking under storm jib and a small mizzen staysail. We were holding a heading of about 340^0, as high as we could point her and would continue on this course for as long as possible; then we would turn on the engine, head west and run straight for Dublin, hoping to put into port by late evening. Our speed was almost six knots, at times reaching seven, subject to the force of the wind. That meant flank-speed, as fast as she would go under sail, being a very heavy boat. It gave us that beautiful, exhilarating feeling that we were doing something absolutely fabulous, foaming through a dark-green, turbulent sea. *Uhuru* had been designed and built as a fishery-assistance-and-protection-vessel for the waters around Iceland, was the epitome of seaworthiness and sailed very dry. She had a lot of buoyancy in the bows and only the odd freak wave would gush some spray over the forecastle. Despite the rough weather this still qualified as a fun-trip in my book. But that was about to change.

Monitoring the emergency frequency we had a receiver on at all times that was tuned to it. That's quite customary. At about 10:25 GMT the SOS came through on the speakers at the helm positions in the wheelhouse and on the flying bridge, partly garbled and a bit hard to understand:

"MAYDAY – MAYDAY - MAYDAY

This is SY Swiftcloude - our position is . . . 52.4252 North and 5.2245 West GPS metric . . ."

It was a woman's voice that made the call, giving the GPS coordinates, repeating the SOS and the coordinates several times. When she ended her transmission this was followed almost instantly by a very calm British man's voice, identifying himself as *HMS Highlander*, acknowledging the SOS and enquiring about the nature of the distress or emergency. From the exchange that followed we learned that the wooden main-mast onboard the sailing yacht *Swiftcloude* had snapped, crashing down into the centre-cockpit and injuring the skipper. The broken mast and tangled mess of rigging and torn sails was blocking access to the deckhouse, locking in the woman who was working their radio and making the distress calls from inside her involuntary prison.

There were four people on board, the injured skipper, presumably with a broken collarbone and possibly some internal injuries, two young men on deck with little sailing experience and the woman in the deckhouse. After a brief pause in transmissions *Highlander* came on again, saying that they had looked into things and considered the situation to be serious. They were too far away to render assistance themselves and were scrambling a Royal Navy SAR Sea King helicopter from Haverford West Aerodrome in Wales straight away, which had happened to be visiting there, ETA at the site of *Swiftcloude* in about twenty minutes. Trevor had already punched the coordinates given by the woman into our GPS and obtained the distance and course to steer to get there.

"They're no more than four nautical miles away." Trevor looked at me. "You reckon we dash over there, just in case? We would arrive at about the same time as the chopper if we go full blast under engine."

“Absolutely!” Paul was already starting the engine, which would give us a top speed of about ten knots.

“New heading is 325^{0}.” Trevor was furling the sails and securing them.

The chopper could get to the three on deck and winch them up but it was unlikely that they carried the kind of equipment on board that they would need to smash their way into the deckhouse to free the woman. It sounded serious.

“Someone may have to get his feet wet.” Trevor was ready for whatever needed to be done.

“Well, being the most expendable I'm the one that's going in while the two of you keep minding the store.” Going over to *Swiftcloude* was really my job.

“Got a plan?”

“I'll take whatever tools I need in our one-man life raft, drift over there, hop aboard *Swiftcloude*, secure the raft, get the woman out and help with the rest of it.”

“Yeah, sounds real easy.” Trevor had been getting bored and welcomed the change of pace.

“OK Trevor, here's what I need: a bolt-cutter, an axe, a torch and an extra survival suit and safety-harness for the woman; also a Very pistol and a handful of red flares, a walkie-talkie, one of those 15-minute oxygen kits and water and a ration-pack, in case pick-up fails and we have to drift all the way to Wales; you never know.” Asking for a ration-pack and water may look like overkill, but we had agreed as standard practice that in emergency situations we would strictly adhere to Murphy's Law, which says that if anything can go wrong, it will, hence prepare for it.

“Consider it done, I'll set up the raft and secure the stuff inside.” Trevor beamed at me. “Why is it always you that gets all the fun action? Is it skipper's privilege?”

“You're right. Who knows, Jack may yet find himself a film-beauty on that yacht, the mysterious prisoner of the wild sea,” with which Paul had us all laughing.

The idea was to position ourselves to windward of *Swiftcloude*, drift backwards towards her stern-to, standing off under engine, and getting as close as we dared.

We came up fast on the site of the disabled yacht just as the Sea King was running in. They circled, most likely to assess the situation and make a plan, figuring out the best way for setting down their Aircrew man, as the Royal Navy likes to call them, Rescue Swimmer or Aviation Survival Technician in the US Coast Guard or man-in-the-water as we called him, the one who was to help getting everybody that needed it winched up.

This would not be easy. The yacht was rocking violently with the swell, listing to port. Part of the mast stuck in the cockpit with what was left of the sails still attached, lots of sail, probably too much, which may be the reason why the mast snapped. There was a tangled mess of rigging, halyards, sheets, broken mast and boom and large chunks of torn sail cloth flapping violently - dangerous if you were hit by it.

It was time to call up the chopper to offer our help, discuss the strategy and divide the workload. "*Rescue helicopter, this is skipper Uhuru*, we're here to assist, over."

"*Uhuru – RN rescue helicopter*, good to see you! State your intentions, over."

"*RN rescue - Uhuru*. We reckon it's too dangerous to winch people off the deck. The cable and boson's chair could get entangled on something, which could even endanger your chopper. I'd say we put a man onboard *Swiftcloude* to get the people into clear, open water from where you could winch them up. We've got a plan. Over."

"*Uhuru – RN rescue*. Sounds good, let's have it." Going by the voice I'd say his rank was that of Commander, someone of authority.

"*RN chopper – Uhuru*." I briefly explained our idea.

"*Uhuru – RN rescue*. Good plan! Go on. Over."

"*RN – Uhuru*. I roger that. Proceeding with plan. Over."

"*Uhuru – RN*. Splendid." The crisp English voice of the presumed commander sounded cheerful. I'm no good at naval ranks, but having listened to him some more I'd bet on him being a commander. "What about you, do we winch you up too when we're all done? Over."

"RN – *Uhuru*. Negative, I'll have to get back to my ship or I'll get court-martialled for going AWOL. Uhuru will go around to leeward of *Swiftcloude*; I'll drift over there and hop onboard when we're all done. Piece of cake. Over." There was a brief and probably puzzled silence; then he got back on:

"*Uhuru – RN rescue*. Are you some kind of military? Over."

"*RN rescue – Uhuru*. Negative, just kidding. Over."

"*RN – Uhuru*. I like your style," he acknowledged with a chuckle. "Let me buy you a drink some day. Proceed, over and out."

"*RN – Uhuru*. Deal,' I said, "let's roll. *Uhuru* out."

We had manoeuvred *Uhuru* backwards up to *Swiftcloude,* with our starboard bow into the wind, getting as close as some fifteen yards. With the raft and gear I drifted across to *Swiftcloude* on her portside, which kept going below the top of the waves, got banged against something but suffered no lasting damage and yelled across to Trevor to let go of the rope once I had cleared the railings. We had briefly considered pulling the four people across to Uhuru in the raft but then agreed that it would be too dangerous, especially getting them up the tall side of the ship, with their skipper being injured and needing immediate medical attention, which we were unable to offer on board *Uhuru.*

On board *Swiftcloude* the two young men looked like frightened rabbits. They could barely hang on to a safe handhold and would be completely useless other than saving themselves - if possible. They eagerly put on my two lifejackets courtesy *Uhuru* as I was quietly wondering why they hadn't been wearing any; maybe the emergency situation had developed rather rapidly. I wanted them off *Swiftcloude* as quickly as possible. I helped them into the water to leeward of *Swiftcloude*, to drift clear on the end of a safety line in case they passed out from the cold, leaving the rest to the chopper.

The injured skipper was in pains but offered to handle the safety line for the two in the water, secured around one of the stanchions. It was hard to communicate with the roaring of the wind and all the rattle and noises from the broken rigging and flapping sails.

"There's . . . in . . . deckhouse . . . get her out . . . hold on . . . safety line . . . boys . . . deckhouse half- flood . . . " he shouted, and I could only catch part of what he said. The ship rocked up and down with the swell.

I had to break into the deckhouse by whatever means possible, banged on the roof with the axe and was pleased when I heard a shout from inside. She was alive, thank God for that. The best way into the deckhouse would be through one of the fairly large panorama windows on the starboard side, which was big enough for a person to crawl through. It was higher above the water level, with the occasional breaker crashing down on it, whilst the port side was already mostly under water, not much time to lose before *Swiftcloude* would go under.

Wearing a survival suit and safety-harness over it, I hooked two snap-on safety lines to a secure point on deck and the free ends to my safety harness, tucked the walkie-talkie away in my breast-pocket and attached the torch and oxygen kit to my belt. Before smashing in the panorama window I tapped the axe against it a couple of times as a signal, hoping that she would stand clear.

A big wave crashed on to the deck the very instant that the window broke, washing me right into the deckhouse, which was already more than hip-deep under water. It was dark inside. I had to struggle to get my bearings and needed a few moments to make out the figure in the yellow oilskins, huddled on to the starboard bench as high up as she could get.

She must have swallowed some water with the breaker and was choking and coughing heavily. I helped her into the survival suit and the safety harness, which I had brought along for her. With water temperature at about eight to ten degrees Celsius the thermal insulation of the survival suit would protect her against the cold as she had to wait in the water while they winched up her husband, and came back for her. I hooked up the second line to her harness, put the oxygen kit in her hand and guided it so that she would find the button to release the oxygen, in case she needed it. The length of the lines kept us by the smashed-in window. When there was a good moment with no water gushing in I pushed her out on to the deck. There was a lot of gear and water was flying in our faces. I needed three tries pulling myself out after her, getting washed back in on the first two occasions.

Then we were both on deck and crawled across to the skipper to put him in the raft as the second of the young men was just being winched into the chopper, making this the perfect moment for going into the water. We floated the raft with the skipper inside overboard on the back of a breaker, both hanging on alongside, drifting to the position where the man-in-the-water was just coming down again on the cable with a stretcher. After they had winched him up, the cable came down again with a boson's chair attached for the woman.

The noise from the rotor and engine of the helicopter above us in addition to that of the storm was deafening. It would have been hard to carry on a conversation. So we didn't try. I hardly got a good look at her with all the oilskins and water gushing in every direction. At the very last moment, as she was being winched up, she turned her head my way and I looked into a very beautiful face with an oriental touch. I must say, there was a kind of magic in the moment, it was moving. She shouted something as she looked down at me, but the wind tore the words from her mouth. I could not take my eyes off her and she, likewise, never turned her eyes away from me, until she was swallowed up by the helicopter. It rose quickly, making headway fast for somewhere east of us."

I took a sip from my cup. "End of story." I said to Harry. There wasn't really anything else to add.

"Wow, what a story. Exciting! How did you get back on board your ship?"

"I hung on to the raft, drifted to where *Uhuru* had been manoeuvred to pick me up, was banged against the side of the ship, and climbed up the scrambling net. Trevor met me halfway to give me a helping hand and pull out the raft. I was back home."

"And the woman, you saw her again, being beautiful, oriental and all that and mysterious?" Harry gave me an inquisitive look. "Surely you would have tried to find her, see her again?"

"I wouldn't recognise her in the street if I saw her again." This was a lie but I wanted to play things down. I would have been too embarrassed to admit to Harry that I had thought of doing just that, going back to find her. But what if I saw her again, being happily married with a husband and a bunch of kids?

"That's hard to believe." Harry persisted. "You must have spent the best part of half an hour, being never more than a foot or two away from her."

"The time from the moment I got on board *Swiftcloude* until she got winched up was no more than ten minutes, at the most, and I wasn't exactly sitting around doing nothing during that time."

"Still an eternity, during which a few friendly words could have been exchanged."

"Well, Harry, there are dos and there are don'ts. She was the yacht skipper's wife. I don't go chasing married women. Anyway, the chopper left in a hurry, to somewhere in the UK. They needed medical attention as a matter of urgency and we had a deadline to meet, getting *Uhuru* into the shipyard in Dublin. Besides, I had to fly back out here the next day, back to work."

I didn't want Harry to ask any more questions, certainly no more personal ones. Like I said before, I don't like talking about myself. So my last words were a bit brisk, bordering on rude and Harry got the drift and left it at that. The last bit of this episode was the part that troubled me. Of course I had got a good look at her. There was an atmosphere of instant closeness between the two of us and a magic, unknown force had implanted, burned, the memory of this event into my emotional system – into my heart.

We both kept silent and had a meal, which Harry had prepared. After the story-telling I needed privacy, to take my mind off something unthinkable, forbidden thoughts. Talking about those dramatic events in the Irish Sea had triggered off a flood of deeply felt emotions, not mere memories, something that gripped me and of which I thought it could not be. I escaped back into my thinking mode, to pursue my private accident investigation into the case of the lost Beaver N66KP, hoping that this would take my mind off the one thought that I did not allow myself to think.

Accidents and Instruments

An assumption is the mother of the screw-up. One of Murphy's never-failing laws.

I wanted to get on with my own investigation of our accident, dealing first with the technical side of this thing. It would be straightforward and I wanted to get it over and done with. Something went bang and broke, the engine stopped running and the flight was terminated then and there. That's all, isn't it? Was there more to it?

Much as we like to think of aviation as an incredibly safe means of transport accidents do, nevertheless, happen, no matter how hard we may try to prevent or avoid them. Therefore, it should not surprise anybody that we have a system to deal with aircraft accidents, which has become standard procedure. Broadly there are three areas on which the attention of the accident investigators will focus. If you deal with these thoroughly and comprehensively you can be sure to have covered everything:

- The man
- the machine and
- the environment in which the accident happened

The combination of all contributing factors that surround an aircraft accident is often referred to as the error chain, a combination of events that ultimately led to the accident. That seemed a well-proven approach, worth following. Whatever may be the reasons, it is generally accepted in the industry as fact that it takes more than one thing to go wrong to bring down an aircraft, resulting in its loss or damage. The first point of the three categories mentioned above deals with the crew. In this case, technically speaking, that was me and nobody else. Harry had been a passenger. I had been in charge and was therefore responsible. Giving an inaccurate position to base was more of an inconvenience, albeit one with potentially terminal consequences for the aircraft's occupants, Harry and myself. It was of peripheral significance, something that happened on the side. It did not qualify as the famous pilot error, the absolute favourite of most aviation authorities, for it makes their subsequent investigation of what went wrong so much easier. A pilot error can be a number of things, ranging from getting lost and hitting the ground to just plain bad flying. In aviation language it is actually a bit pompously called 'controlled flight into terrain'. None of this had been the case. Nevertheless, I heaped recrimination on my head for at least two serious errors of judgment, which is no more and no less than admitting to some kind of pilot error.

The first one was to even have thought of involving Harry in the navigational aspects of the flight, doing the flight following. For this he had the map and the onboard instruments. He had to monitor our progress from A to B to the point of being able to say at any time with some degree of certainty where we were. As transpired later Harry made a mistake in figuring out our position. He relayed this information to base by making radio calls every twenty minutes. This had nothing to do with triggering off whatever it was that went wrong inside the engine compartment. But it did have certain consequences and I would need to question the wisdom of letting Harry do the flight following.

The other and more serious error on my part had been to agree to work for the Karibak Pipeline Company in the first place. Maybe I am allowing some of my frustration with the Company's way of doing things to cloud my judgment. They did perform all necessary maintenance, as prescribed and laid down in the various manuals and kept the aircraft in an airworthy condition, technically speaking. Was I looking for more?

The finger of suspicion clearly pointed at a serious technical fault in the aircraft or some of its vital equipment, which had failed. There was every indication that this was what we were dealing with in this case. When things go bang, engine or aircraft parts fly through the air and the engine quits, this ceases to be a matter of opinion or philosophy. The facts speak for themselves:

The Event:

Technical failure that resulted in an in-flight engine shut-down with an ensuing uncontained engine fire, presumed to be from a disintegrated fuel pump or ruptured fuel line.'

That is the kind of language that would set the tone of the inevitable accident report, which someone would write once they had looked at all the evidence they could find. And the environment? A contributing factor to the end result, the destruction of the aircraft, had been the fact that we had to fly so low beneath the base of the clouds that we did not have sufficient altitude to glide to a safe location, to set the aircraft down once we lost power. But in the Error Chain this would rank among the consequences, not something that caused the crash. Although the weather had been bad, if not outright awful, there was absolutely no indication that this would have had anything to do with whatever went bang up front. I was quite satisfied that outside interference of any kind did not trigger off the sequence of events that led to the unscheduled landing in rough terrain.

For the time being that completed the picture. The cause was technical, the man-aspect would get further attention and the environment was declared by me to have been innocent. That left the secondary aspects. Were there any contributing factors once the forced landing was unavoidable? I had two things on my mind. The first one was the question of whether I could have landed the aircraft more or less intact. The landing had been what we like to call 'a controlled crash'. When disaster had struck I had been grateful to be flying a tail-dragger. With a tricycle landing gear, as is common in modern aircraft, the nose-wheel would have dug itself in on first impact and would have caused the aircraft to flip over on contact with the ground, with the aircraft careening along on its back and us dangling in our seat harnesses, upside down or worse.

In that respect our tail-dragger had saved us. Once on the ground we had run out of luck. We had had no choice and simply had to set down where the apple falls, in a manner of speaking, not on smooth ground. The flight had not ended on anything that even remotely resembled a runway but between rock outcrops sticking out of the ice and snowdrifts and we had been unable to avoid hitting things so that the aircraft broke up.

So far, so bad, plain bloody bad luck.

The other secondary aspect was the broad subject of air navigation, in particular the obvious screw-up about our position reporting, the flight following that would have put base in a position to pick us up in a matter of hours, if they had known where we were.

Modern aircraft have an impressive array of navigational instruments, the most glamorous one of which is the Global Positioning System or GPS. It is basically a combination of radio receiver and computer. The receiver picks up certain data from satellites circling overhead, courtesy of the US government and the computer works out where you are, give or take a small margin of error, which the Pentagon has factored into the system, in order to prevent its use for sinister purposes.

With the advent of the GPS grid maps had become obsolete. Nowadays it would be much easier to simply read off and relay to base the coordinates of your actual position that the GPS will display at the pushing of a button. But because of its low priority status in the company the old Beaver did not have a GPS.

Instead we had to rely on the traditional aviator's skills. There are three things that determine the progress of your flight relative to a point of departure: aircraft course, speed and any movement of the air that surrounds you. If the air is still, i. e. there is no wind, this is zero and all that counts is course and speed. If there is wind that means the air that surrounds you is moving relative to the ground and your progress is affected. This is not reflected by what compass and air speed indicator tell you. There are ways and means of knowing this and taking it into account, you compensate for head, tail or crosswind. That is the part that obviously had eluded Harry.

Having for whatever reasons failed to report an accurate position to base brought the focus of attention back to the question of the ELT, the Emergency Location Transmitter, which on our aircraft had been u/s, 'un-serviceable', or more precisely totally useless. The blasted thing had been broken even before we took off! That had meant no homing signal to guide potential rescuers. I was tempted to say 'of course!' If all else goes wrong, why stop here. But that would have been cynical.

All things considered we were still alive and had nothing to bitch about. If ours had been a passenger revenue flight our company Minimum Equipment List, the MEL, would not have allowed us to do the flight; no ifs and buts. If you fly people through the landscape you want to be able to find them as quickly as possible, if anything goes wrong.

The fact that our MEL was not overly concerned about finding the crew of a missing otherwise empty aircraft should go a long way towards explaining how the lives of pilots are viewed in the industry: we are expendable. We have been reduced to being mere insurance items, albeit at times potentially lucrative ones: one aircraft sadly lost with crew onboard. Too bad, tough luck!

"Get a letter off to Lloyd's, Cathy, about the aircraft and that key-man-insurance. And put an ad into *Aviation Week* for some pilots."

One sunny summer afternoon some time before this event I had had an experience that underscores the potential usefulness of the ELT in finding a downed aircraft. Relaxing in a deck chair outside Operations I had been on call at base, waiting for something to happen. Something soon did. A large US Coast Guard helicopter approached slowly, almost hesitantly and started circling around the maintenance area in ever decreasing circles, finally homing in on the main hangar. After hovering over it for an instant the helicopter pulled away and landed about twenty yards from where I had put my book under a piece of rock, to stop it from being blown away by the rotor wash. Two men in full flight kit jumped out and one of them came up to me.

"You guys got a wreck in the hangar?"

"No, not that I know of."

"Well, we're picking up an ELT; let's go and check it out." I got out of my chair and we marched across a stretch of tarmac to the side entrance of the main hangar. There was only one aircraft inside, one of the company's DC-3s. The one who had first spoken to me, a young lieutenant in an orange-coloured flight suit, pressed down a button on his left-hand breast pocket, like Mr. Spock and all the others of the *Enterprise* and talked into the chin microphone that was attached to his helmet, obviously to someone they left behind in the helicopter.

"Say, Hank, you still got that ELT?"

"Sure do. Hang on, I'll give you a fix." A few seconds went by and we could hear him again over the tiny loudspeaker on the lieutenant's breast pocket. "I got it for you, I'd say, give or take a little, about ten yards clockwise from where you're standing."

The lieutenant turned to me again. "It's in the tail, is it, I mean the ELT on that aircraft?"

"Sure, I could have told you so. No need to trouble your mate."

As soon as I said it I realised that I was not in any position to give our friends from the USCG a lot of lip. If the ELT on our DC-3 was transmitting they had clearly caught us on an infringement of the rules. You're not supposed to operate your ELT for more than thirty seconds at a time, when you are testing it. Anything else may be seen as an emergency transmission and you are responsible for the cost, if anybody comes to rescue you when, in fact, you are just sitting there, steadying your right hand by holding on to a can of Miller Light and listening to your portable radio, taking a break from some demanding repair job.

The Lieutenant shot me a look, not the kind that is meant to kill you, just to show displeasure, but emphatically and with the full weight of authority that only a government can bestow on people in its service.

We climbed inside the aircraft to see if perhaps accidentally somebody had turned on the switch with which the ELT could be activated, for instance if you want to test it and see if it works. I remembered that Bob Masters had carried out some inspection on the aircraft in the morning. I lifted the lid of the protective casing, found the switch, unfortunately, in the 'ON' position, and turned it off.

The lieutenant gave us the full works. "What you got now, Hank?"

"Hold a sec . . . eh . . . zilch. It's off." The voice of the invisible man came back over the suit speaker. Inwardly green with envy I took the opportunity to admire the beautiful equipment that the Coast Guard issued its staff.

Of course, I thought but kept my mouth shut. It was time to do some soft soaping, damage control. I tried to look casual, closed the lid and said, "You guys care for some coffee?"

"Well, let's get this matter settled first." The other man, a sergeant, took the floor. "You realise that's an infringement?"

“Yeah, sure. Look, I’m sorry. I guess we screwed up. It wasn’t intentional, you know.”

The Coast Guard people were still pretty annoyed at having had their time and the US taxpayer’s fuel thus wasted. But eventually they accepted the coffee, as a kind of common courtesy, after I suggested that our company coffee was so lousy that it could not possibly be seen as a bribe, but should rather be considered as a ‘stand-off weapon’. Using this kind of stilted, pseudo-military language made everybody laugh, breaking the ice. But it still took a lot of pleading to stop them from writing up a formal report and complaint which, in due course, would have been followed by a bill from Uncle Sam for ‘Rescue Services Rendered’. And then Bob Masters would have had to do some explaining to the accountants. Lucky escape!

Whilst it may have been gratifying to know that these gadgets really work, they are strictly reserved for emergencies. In this case, the Coast Guard had picked up the signal from over fifteen miles away and rushed to the site of the presumed crash. It had been extremely embarrassing. The long and the short of it is, if our ELT had worked, finding us would have been the notorious piece of cake.

Just to wrap this up and while we are digressing, the famous Black Box cannot go unmentioned. Whenever there is news on television of a plane crash in remote or inaccessible areas, say in the jungles of Africa or South America or into the sea, someone will refer to the search for the aircraft’s Black Box, with the suggestion that once this is found the cause of the crash and the events leading to it can be suitably explained. There are actually two Black Boxes: the Flight Data Recorder or FDR, connected with the aircraft’s most important flight control and navigational instruments and the Cockpit Voice Recorder or CVR, which records all conversations inside the cockpit and radio broadcasts between the crew and the outside world. Both Black Boxes are protected by very solid fire, water-pressure and shock-proof casings. The colour of the outer casing of the Black Boxes is actually orange, to make them easier to find. I would hazard a wild guess that the adjective ‘black’ in the name was, most likely, inspired by typical aviator’s superstition and the very common, firm belief in some form or other of black magic surrounding the fate of some aircraft lost under mysterious circumstances.

Both the Flight Data and the Cockpit Voice Recorder usually bring no direct or immediate benefit to an aircraft's crew, even if they are among the lucky survivors. They are strictly for posterity under the heading of 'Lessons to be Learned', important as that may be. The requirement to carry those instruments on board may vary with aircraft size and mission type, but they are usually mandatory in conjunction with commercial aviation.

Having already drawn a blank on the ELT we should not be too surprised to learn that our little Beaver did not have any Black Boxes on board, nor was there any requirement to carry them. But even if we had had them, their presence would not have made the slightest difference to our immediate actions following our little disaster. But this is where we ought to draw a line.

The aviation industry largely works on the infamous need-to-know principle, a management concept which is based on never telling people any more than one absolutely has to. Thus when circumstances change and things come to the crunch, you know absolutely nothing and hence become totally useless. On that basis I have already said more than was absolutely necessary, save for this: the even worse second principle is called negative reporting.

"If you don't hear from me by ten o' clock that means we're right on track."

Really? What if our man falls off his bicycle or under a bus before he can make that phone-call or otherwise? The point is that with negative reporting you haven't got a clue as to what is really happening. Fortunately, negative reporting is on the way out. But it still happens. Whom am I telling? Like with our little disaster. Harry reported something and thought I was listening, which I was not. I was daydreaming and thought Harry was giving correct location data to base. That is a bad case of dual negative reporting. We had been assuming things, both ways around and should have known better, for in more enlightened circles of the aviation world people hold to the belief that assumption is the mother of the screw-up. In other words: never assume anything unless it is confirmed and then you know it, don't have to guess. If we had been in the military,

Harry would have said to me: "I'm now going to report our position at so-and-so." I would have listened to it and given my OK.

That realisation didn't look so good for me and put the focus of my attention back on looking at the man who had been in charge of flying Beaver N66KP; none other than myself.

The Moment of Truth

There is no difference between 'instincts' and 'gut feeling'!'

It was time to focus on the one remaining human link in the chain, the pilot of the aircraft. Had he been fit to fly? Did he do anything that he should not or not do something that he should have done? Would the end-result have been different if somebody else had flown the aircraft? Did the responsibility for the flight and its eventual outcome lie with somebody else altogether?

I had definitely been fit to fly. There wasn't a thing to suggest otherwise. About the responsibility for the flight there was also no question. It is true that somebody else ordered the flight to take place. But that order and its subsequent implementation went through the normal channels of an air operation.

That was where I had come in. I had accepted the aircraft for the flight and signed Al Hickman's release papers, which had got him off and me on the hook. I had accepted the aircraft in as-is, where-is condition, fly-away-Camp-Bravo. This would have been the legal definition, more or less in these words. That clearly placed the responsibility for accepting to conduct the flight in my court.

Did I have reasonable cause to reject the aircraft on the grounds of available evidence when I accepted it? I came to the conclusion that there had been nothing tangible to suggest that there were any unusual circumstances. Everybody knew that the aircraft had been in storage. It is also common knowledge that long periods of aircraft storage may lead to some form or other of corrosion. I did not recall having any hard information which I then disregarded. There was nothing that I could have done but accept the aircraft and fly. That notion helped me to deal with this issue in a definitive manner and I thought I could dismiss this point as irrelevant. Suddenly I remembered that I had been at Camp Bravo at an earlier date when someone worked on the Beaver, connecting the fuel pump.

"Hey, Cliff, you looked inside that pump?"

"What for? It's been reconditioned, sitting on the shelf for as long as I can remember. Well - I guess they did have it out and on the airplane for about twenty hours and took it off the airplane again."

"Why?"

"Who the hell knows?"

Cliff went on to install that pump and I walked away and forgot all about this little scene. Maybe my subconscious mind remembered it when I accepted the aircraft. But the conscious part of me did not. Was there an element of doubt in the back of my head about the maintenance status of the Beaver? Or was all I had just the general aviator's superstition, which had somehow graduated to a gut feeling, no more? At any rate that would not have been good enough to refuse the flight.

I was arriving at a difference in significance between *gut feeling* and *basic instinct.* But I could not leave it there. How do you tell the difference? Maybe I was too quick in dismissing the gut feeling as something of a lesser order. Perhaps we have to look for something to do with the intensity of the warning that is being transmitted through your subconscious mind and the way in which it mysteriously reaches into your sphere of conscious awareness. Maybe the case did after all deserve to be taken a step further.

And then it hit me with a bang. I should have refused the flight! Yes, I should have trusted my instincts and had not. My subconscious inner voice came through loud and clear: stop mincing words and fidgeting around. If you want to survive, trust me! That is what I should have done and came up with the following:

Verdict (Version One):

Subject man (that's me) overruled gut feeling and accepted aircraft. It subsequently transpired that a rejection would have been justified, given the eventual end result, i. e. fuel pump failure, premature termination of the mission and aircraft loss, endangering the lives of the aircraft's occupants.

That reduced this particular issue to finding the reason 'why' an experienced pilot ignored his gut feeling and that something was wrong. I listed that under 'investigate further', maybe together with other items, the things I should have done and didn't and vice-versa. Were they part of the same deal, the same underlying pattern? I needed to look at that more closely.

I could dismiss the question as to what would have happened if anybody else had flown the aircraft. That would be the kind of speculation and conjecture that does not get you anywhere. We have come to accept certain things in daily life.

I was a duly qualified pilot, it was my turn to take on the job and the company and I had followed accepted procedures as laid down in the company's Maintenance and Operations Manuals, as approved by the FAA. Looking at things the 'book way', as in 'doing it by the book', my actions in accepting the aircraft and taking on the flight had been correct as per the very letter of the book.

And then it was clear to me: my inner voice had shouted a warning and I had disregarded it and gone on to do the flight. The aircraft's engine had failed, book or no book. And I am saying that following my gut feeling could have prevented that? Maybe. That made the reason why I had not followed the inner voice all the more important, which brought me back to the things that I should or should not have done: Why did I override my basic instinct or mere gut feeling about accepting the aircraft? Did my obvious failure to supervise Harry's flight following contribute to the loss of the aircraft and the consequences?

Whether I liked it or not, I was now looking at something that was pretty serious. Even though I knew that whatever Harry did or did not do had nothing to do with the fact that the explosion in the aircraft's engine compartment took place, my total lack of interest in what he did was unacceptable on the grounds of principle: either you have a professionally run operation or you don't. Either I let Harry do the flight following and made sure he got it right or I treated him as the passenger that he was, technically speaking, and did the flight following myself - properly, of course, of that I had no doubt. It would have been child's play for me. This still left the question of why I acted the way I did.

Cherchez la femme!

When you cannot think of anything else, look for a woman on whom you can pin it!

Why had it taken me so long? It was obvious why I had not listened to my aviator's inner voice: I had listened to another inner voice, albeit one that was functioning on a different level, one that was perhaps elemental, if you placed the magic powers of love at the forefront of your objective in life, with little or no concern for your own survival: The two basic instincts had competed with each other.

Was that possible and if so, why? Rationality intervened and told me that something here was out of line. You cannot follow the voice of love, the ultimate - most times undisclosed - objective of which is to happily contribute to the continuation of the species, if you die before you get a chance to do so. In other words, flying through life on the wings of love is pointless if you kill yourself before you reach the one to whom you are so forcefully attracted.

Yuko!

The brains part had given me a distinctly uneasy feeling - to the point that my subconscious self saw the mission as being endangered. It knew that the aircraft's fuel pump had been sitting on a shelf for so many years, whether reconditioned or not,

The other part, the emotional side, had pushed all concern and anxiety from my mind with the clear instruction: 'Come on, mate, your lunch with Yuko is coming up. Why are you hesitating, why all that fussing and dithering? Do you want to spend the next forty-eight hours at Camp Bravo, missing out on the one true highlight of your present life that would make you forget all the solitude of the last ten years? Wasn't that precisely the kind of highlight that made life worth living? Get on with it! Get yourself a life, before it is too late!'

Something inside me had rearranged my priorities. The flame of desire, burning desire, deep longing, passion, affection and love had triumphed over the urge to survive! I had acted with total disregard for whatever consequences might ensue! For a man like me, the predominantly rational, cool, calm, thinking type that was tantamount to an act of utter and unwarranted irrationality.

The love bug had overridden the traditional side of the man. Not just once. Accepting the flight was one thing. But look at what had happened during the flight, how I had totally disregarded Harry's radio communications with base. If he had given them a position that was light-years off course, I would not have noticed it, for I was not functioning rationally anymore, at least not on that particular level.

The second instinct had clearly outperformed the first and, as I had always believed, most elemental one. Passion, desire and longing had triumphed over the ingrained will to live. This was not only highly illogical, but also impossible, as long as I thought about it rationally. But I had stopped doing that.

Alas!

So that is how it had worked. The forces of passion and desire had triumphed on that fateful day. When it comes to the crunch, you disregard all else and follow the one inner voice that matters more to you: either survival, or love.

Slowly the truth started to filter through to my rational mind. It did not just happen to the birds, the bees and the butterflies! It happened to rational men, serious professionals, highly trained and very experienced aviators. I was human after all, subjected to the same basic forces that have determined man's actions ever since he came out of his cave or fell off the family tree. The final realisation was both sobering and reassuring, as I drew the ultimate conclusions of what had happened.

Verdict – Version Two:

Subject man failed to recognise intuitive danger signals, concerning the airworthiness of the aircraft and take action commensurate therewith, i. e. reject the aircraft and cancel the flight. Subsequently, when the flight was in progress, he diverted his conscious attention from communications and thereby flight safety related matters, leading up to serious procedural errors that remained unnoticed. As a consequence, the aircraft's actual true position was unknown at the Company's Base. The eventual rescue effort was thereby severely hampered and put in jeopardy, unnecessarily.

Well, let's face it. It was nice and comforting to know that I was human after all. But it was also blatantly clear that I had yet to clean up my emotional infrastructure. Love is a beautiful fact of life. But if you are the pilot of an aircraft with responsibility for lives and equipment, you have got to sort yourself out in such a way that your rational functioning is not impaired.

Let us get this straight. If you are the passenger on an aircraft or, for that matter, a train or a bus, before you trust them with your life and allow them to depart, do you first go and ask the guy up front, "say, mister, is your love life in order?"

How crude!

And out of place. Something here is not right. We have to dig a little deeper than we have been doing, a whole lot deeper. We've got to go back to the root of the problem, turned disaster, back to the origins of whatever it was that led to such irrational and illogical conduct by someone who's got four stripes on his sleeve and a paper in his pocket that says that he is a responsible citizen, one that can be entrusted with the piloting of aircraft 'for hire or reward'. Before we shake the foundations of what we deem to be the essentials of our daily working life, the secure knowledge that things are what they are meant and seem to be and that people are who they are supposed to be, we have got to go back to the very bottom of the affair, to the point in the man's life, my life, where things started going wrong.

Louise

'. . . a slowly growing love, not realized'

Lydia and I did not have much time to sit around and mope. Before we knew we came under enormous pressure to get on with our lives. Because of my added responsibility in view of raising a family I left my salaried job to set up my own engineering firm. This in turn triggered off a vicious cycle of needing more staff to do the work, more money to pay the extra staff, more work, which required more staff etc. This should be enough to outline the principle. It was a no-win scenario.

You continue to fight an uphill battle, also known as the young entrepreneur's death spiral. I was chronically undercapitalised, understaffed and overworked. Before we ourselves noticed it, we evolved into what people came to look upon as a 'lovely family', with two beautiful children, two Mercedes cars, a Swiss au-pair, a part-time kitchen help and a steadily increasing bank overdraft.

We had every reason to be grateful. The kids were doing well at school; nobody was into drugs or stealing cars - or bicycles, before they were old enough to be doing the cars. That was a whole lot better than many another family was doing. Lydia continued to receive a lot of praise and acclaim and I was commonly referred to as 'the husband of that delightful and charming young woman from Cairo, or Beirut', depending on what people actually knew about her.

On a personal level I benefited from the fact that I had absolutely no time to think about my own problems or feel sorry for myself. Sometimes, when sleep would not come, although the body was exhausted, the mind wandered off into a fantasyland, seeking warmth, comfort, emotional shelter and, from time to time, an imagined shoulder to cry on.

I was surviving – emotionally – in the head, in a world from which I had banished all feelings in favour of the semblance of peace and tranquillity. That got me through the days, one at a time.

In her own particular way Lydia was the perfect wife, reliable, loyal and obedient. It is never quite right. I was longing for a partner, someone with whom I could discuss my innermost problems, the things that moved me. That was the dream. A partner does not obey, does not have to and I did not look for obedience in my woman. A partner bonds with you, your minds fuse, you learn to function as an entity. No need for obedience!

But there I reached into empty space. Lydia simply was not accessible on that level. In fairness to her it has to be said that she had no family history of husband and wife partnerships. She did not know what a partnership of this kind was, therefore did not miss it. Her concept was a clear understanding of the roles that each of the two had to perform, in particular her part, which she took on to perfection. She handled it the way she saw it, not necessarily my way, but one for which she got a lot of approval all round.

I was the one who was different.

As a consequence I continued to be alone, alone in the middle of a family of four. The upside was that she never even attempted to interfere with anything that I wanted to do, the downside that I had to do it alone. In a sense I now had three kids, sometimes four, if you included the au pair, who was traded in for next year's model once a year, meaning that we had to retrain them when they were just beginning to get the hang of things.

All that will sound like the typical, ungrateful male chauvinist's outlook on suburban life, as was the fact that I had an obedient wife, but not a friend and lover. How could I? Where and when should she have developed that side? From her father, who obviously believed in arranged marriages under the 'Daddy knows best' scenario? Not bloody likely!

I could not escape the fact that I felt increasingly lonely, alone, left alone, left to my own devices with a lot of responsibility and not an awful lot of rewards. All I really did in life was move back and forth between home and the office, usually during the hours of darkness, early morning one way, back the other way late evening or at night.

How she really felt deep down inside remained her secret. I did not have a way of reaching into her inner sphere, the same as she did not reach into mine, nor did she appear to try. As I was getting increasingly unhappy so was she. While she was better at keeping her true feelings locked up inside I did not have a clue as to what was going on inside that head of hers. I sensed that she was disappointed and unhappy, but her austere upbringing had conditioned her for that. Maybe it was even accepted by her as a normal part of a woman's life. So, whatever it may have been, she never complained but suffered through it.

'This stupid bastard should thank the Lord on his knees for the wife he got!' I hear people say, it could have been much worse. That is absolutely right and the reason why it lasted so long and in the way that it did. It should not come as too much of a surprise that our relationship did not stand out as a particularly romantic one. You would have looked in vain for any eroticism in it, which just would not have been part of her outlook on life. I think deep down inside she came to regard sexuality, male sexuality, my male sexuality with a certain degree of contempt. Far from ever even remotely trying to seduce me sexually, nobody would accuse her of having showered me with openly expressed affection, let alone any form of tenderness, whilst I was longing, aching to express the deep felt tenderness that was running through every fibre of my physical existence. Like fish need water, I longed for it to become part of my life. But it did not. Lydia did not communicate with me in that sphere.

Increasingly I settled into this harsh reality of life, resigning myself to the fact that there were things that would be out of reach for me. I accepted the fact that I had nobody but myself to blame for this. When I should have got my priorities right, my head was in Camelot while my heart and soul were in dreamland. Headlong I had stormed off into a world high on principle and ethical demands of the noblest order, but low on emotional truthfulness.

I had asked for it and I had got it.

After a dozen years of twelve to fifteen-hour days at work I reached the point where my inner systems were on the brink of collapse. The workload alone was not so bad. Telling myself I was doing it for a good cause was something which I could learn to accept. It was the loneliness that was getting to me. My original vision of married life had been one where the young couple creates a new family. But as her disappointment began to take a firmer hold of her, Lydia began to see herself more and more consciously and noticeably in the role of her father's daughter, returning to the one male role model in her life that was and would forever continue to be perfect.

At first I had thought I had imagined it. But the telltale signs were increasingly apparent, when she no longer tried to conceal her disappointment. Eventually that became clear to me, compounding my perceived state of isolation, coupled with a sense of despair. I was as alone as I had ever been. And I had brought it upon myself with the determination and vigour that one normally associates with mountain climbers: Just reach the top, no matter how or why.

"How wonderful, Jack, we were just talking about you! Louise is here with her husband. Won't you come around for some of my delicious cake?"

I had obtained a project that on occasion required trips to southern France. This was the second such trip after the project had started. Sitting in my hotel room, wondering what to do with the rest of a perfectly good April day in southern France, without thinking and as if in autopilot-mode I had dialled Louise's telephone number, the one at her parents' house. It was the only one that I knew for her, remembering it as if I had been dialling it every day.

I was surprised when her mother answered the phone, surprised that anybody answered it and even more at what her mother said to me. It only took an instant and I was in the car, driving to that lovely house in the country that I had visited so many times and which I could have found blindfolded, if necessary.

It had been a young man who had last visited it, someone without a care in the world, eagerly running towards his sweetheart. Now I felt apprehensive and was afraid, not knowing why. I would see Louise again, after all this time, Louise with a husband and quite probably a bunch of kids. After all, it had been so many years in which I had completely removed her from my conscious mind, never thinking of her.

We had not come face to face for more than a brief moment, just long enough for the 'hellos', 'how do you do' for the husband and a few words of greetings for her mother, when Louise under some pretext beckoned me to go outside with her, saying something that must have made a lot of sense to everybody in the room, for nobody raised the slightest objection. But even if you marched me in front of a firing squad I could not remember what went on during those brief moments except that suddenly we were alone and in each other's arms, driven together by a force so powerful and inescapable as I had never experienced before.

It was not just me, it was both of us. That great, mysterious force had taken hold of both of us and locked us into an embrace so intense and powerful and yet so tender, that our surroundings and the passage of time dissolved into an eternity of endless space. We had become part of a limitless universe and nothing else around us mattered any more. I could feel the intensity of Louise's emotions that pulsed into my body as much as my feelings swept over her like a breaker crashing onto the seashore. For those precious, timeless moments we had become one. Our minds, hearts and souls had fused into a common state of being, where the boundaries of the individual are dissolved, blending into a sea of love and passion, full of desire and yet so gentle. For that brief, beautiful, immeasurable moment Louise and I had erased the time that lay between us since our last encounter, as if we had never left each other's arms. We had returned to a time that for both of us had meant happiness.

It had been a slowly growing love, not realised.

When we rejoined the family I began to pick up vibes, feelings and emotions that were running through the room. The atmosphere between Louise and her husband was tense, bordering on signs of rudeness and mutual contempt that one sees so often in marriages where the fire has gone out, that are held together by the often compelling and unforgiving forces of convention or expediency.

Louise's mother openly mused about what would have happened if Louise and I had got married instead. I only realised then that I might have missed more than one clue at the time, when some vital, albeit unconscious decisions were made. We found a quiet, unobserved moment to agree that we had to meet again, alone, without all the entourage. It was apparent that this was absolutely necessary for the peace of mind of both of us, even for our sanity, hers just as much as mine.

Louise's husband, a successful and obviously important doctor, had to return to Paris that same evening, where they lived.

Louise and I met the next day.

We spent one glorious day together, immersed in a spirit of sheer happiness, outright joy. I had never felt so good in my whole life, I could have screamed out loud. We went to our favourite spot where we had spent so many harmonious moments when we were just school kids, enjoying the shy and tender closeness of innocent, young love, even if we never called it that, not knowing at the time what it was. If anybody asked us we answered that we were 'going together'.

We had difficulty recognising the place. Where there had been just shrubs and bushes there were trees now, as a quiet and solemn reminder of the effects of the passage of so many years, years that we had spent without each other. That one day was absolute heaven without a care in the world, sheer happiness, experienced by both of us. We hardly talked; content to hold each other in a warm and tender embrace, surrendering to the flood of emotions of love, warmth, affection and pure passion. We did not make any plans. But we agreed to meet again in Amsterdam in three weeks' time. She would state as a reason the desire to go and see the Rembrandt Collection at the Rijksmuseum, which made sense because she was getting into art history. I did not need any reason other than that I wanted to see her.

When we met again later in Amsterdam as agreed and planned, reality had caught up with us. It did not take us long to start talking. That was when the despair and sadness set in. You cannot turn back the wheels of time, it is just not possible. We looked for options but there weren't any. Neither of us was prepared to make any radical move at that time. Much as we wanted each other, no plan emerged. I had a notion that we should bring about a friendship, which was to include our partners, denying ourselves the fulfilment of passion and desire.

It was an ambitious and foolish plan. And, of course, it did not work. We arranged for everybody to meet socially, which turned into the closest thing to a human relations disaster that I have ever come across. Although Lydia and I had long ago moved apart, each occupying different parts of the house, sexual contacts having ceased, that had no bearing on her attitude to the venture. She was upset like I had never seen her before. For the first time ever in our relationship she showered me with reproach. How could I do this to her? As if I had deliberately engineered some sinister plot. Why did I marry her if I loved another woman? I did not know I did. Had I no respect for her parents whom she had left for me? I had not ever even thought about that. Well, and so on.

There were lots of tears and whatever belief in me she might still have had was shattered then and there. She did not help me to sort out my emotional dilemma. She could not, for she was unable to see that I was experiencing a dilemma, a true and profound dilemma of feelings, emotions, loyalties and my deeply rooted sense of commitment to her and our children, regardless of everything else. She had never learned to manage her emotions, deal with emotional issues of any kind and the only tools she had at her disposal were principles of conduct in life, which I had so shamelessly and selfishly violated.

It soon became clear to Louise and me that there was no nice and simple solution to our situation, which was not to say that there was any solution at all. Avoiding a decision or decisive action of any kind we resorted to letter writing and never met again, save for one more time, which was in public. The letters were a clandestine operation with her cousin acting as our intermediary, whenever one was needed. Louise had given my letters to the cousin for safe keeping. When she told her to throw them in the trash, all this ground to an abrupt end. Maybe she had done it on the spur of the moment, maybe for fear of not being able to handle things any more.

Whatever were the reasons, the effect that this had on me was abrupt and decisive. It broke the spell that had bonded Louise and me together. The relationship, sadly, ended then and there, three years after that fateful day in April, when I had followed the invitation to sample her mother's cake, three years after my one day of happiness.

Lydia and I had split up and I made a significant career change to become a professional pilot, getting rid of my company, which had increasingly turned into a never-ending hard slog with no friendly shore in sight.

"Hey, Jack old boy . . . you still there? You haven't said a word for hours." Indeed, I had not, for I had been so wrapped up in my memories, forgetting all about where I was and how and why this had come about. Harry was sitting up on his bunk, looking at me. "You had that far away look on your face." He said it more like a question than a statement, as if he were trying to nudge me on into telling him what I was thinking about.

"Yeah, Harry, long ago and far away. I was in another land, another time. Memories. You telling me your story started me on doing my own thinking. I couldn't help it, it just came over me."

"That's all right, old boy, no need to make excuses. I'm glad to see that there exists a touch of humanity behind that impenetrable professional front of yours."

I could tell that he had not said it to offend me. It was the way he regarded me: As the somewhat impersonal, immovable and outwardly cold and equally dedicated aviation man.

"Harry, if it is any consolation to you, I was lost in thought about happier times, also some less happy ones and a lot of things that I wished I hadn't done and some that I wished I had."

"Wow! That bad! And I thought I had problems!"

"It's not problems, Harry. It's more like suddenly having opened the floodgates to memories that I had suppressed for such a long time, things you either did not want to remember or that hurt so much that you had pushed them aside, banned into a dark corner, labelled 'things not to be pulled to the surface'."

This was the first time I had expressed any kind of feelings towards Harry, having been a distant and reserved listener up to now. From one moment to the next I had opened up to him, dropping my guard, giving him an insight into my inner state of being, a first glimpse.

"You also have a mysterious history?" Harry looked at me, openly, fairly and squarely. Honestly. He conveyed a sense of being sincere, which made me feel good.

"I was thinking of when and where I really screwed up in every single one of my personal relationships and what it did to me." I said it without hesitation, but then I felt that I was not ready to talk to Harry above and beyond what I had already said. Not yet. Maybe it would come. And Harry impressed me, now more than ever before, by showing me that he was a very caring and tactful soul. There would come a moment, when I would have to tell Harry how truly sorry I was for having been such a pompous sonofabitch as to treat him in the high-handed manner that I had been doing. Something here was suddenly becoming apparent, something that I would need to do above and beyond coming to terms with whatever was eating me up inside.

I needed to reconcile my inner state of being with the rest of the world and for all intents and purposes Harry was now that rest of the world. He was representing the outside world and this was the first time in my life that I had ever revealed my feelings to anybody, the first time ever.

I could not remember ever before having expressed any kind of feelings to anybody else, maybe Louise, but I could not remember any specific moment or occasion. My mind had gone blank in that respect.

That bad. Yeah, I thought, that bad. Harry, without consciously trying to do anything, had shown me the most fundamental shortcoming in my conduct of life: My inability to communicate with anybody, be they loved ones or partners, friends or strangers.

Late. Yes, it was late, but not too late for me to realise that life and living means dealing with people, not just oneself. And dealing with people means to communicate with them, which in turn is a two-way process, listening and talking, receiving and giving, accepting and conveying. I still had a long way to go.

Did the wolves out there in that wilderness communicate? Come to think of it I bet they did!

Seeing the Light

Sadness and joy. You have to go through such an awful lot of one in order to experience just a tiny bit of the other

It was now pitch dark inside the cabin and I was grateful for it. I needed to shut Harry out of my personal sphere, once again, maybe just this one more time. Now that things were finally coming together, falling into place, I needed to be alone with myself. Something was on my chest, troubling me in the form of a reminder that I had some unfinished business. I wanted to put an end to that, get on with my life and sort out whatever it was that needed sorting out. My undivided attention was required. I needed to think straight.

Earlier Harry had insisted on fixing dinner, which had consisted of some canned food and tea. I had been impatient, could not finish soon enough, so that I could finally be alone with my thoughts and my sadness that was easier to bear when you were alone. It is such an elemental state of being, close, intimate, personal and honest, but above all inescapable and indivisible. It was something that affected you and nobody else and you and nobody else had to deal with it.

Now, again, I was overcome by that deep, heartfelt sadness that was stronger than any other feeling that I had ever experienced - except that one day in my life, when I had felt nothing but joy, total and absolute joy, when nothing else had mattered, when Louise and I had spent that one delightful and unforgettable day in April in the countryside in southern France.

Sadness and joy; you have to go through such an awful lot of one in order to experience just a tiny bit of the other. And yet, would we really understand and grasp those rare moments of joy, if it were not for all the sadness, the loneliness? It was time to put together the pieces of the jigsaw puzzle that was the architecture of my inner state of being, my past emotional life and its effects.

I had meant so well. Maybe that was the problem. It had come from the mind, the head and whatever it is that we associate with it, the power to determine and control our actions. The result of our deeds and actions is our footprint, the tracks we leave as we go through life, the kind of splash that we make in the big pond, whether it is just ripples, waves or an outright storm or hurricane.

The head, our intellect, the consciously responsible part of our personality, has a limited choice of tools on which to base decisions and actions: Knowledge, acquired skills, experience and information. There are all the things that we perceive and have compiled in our memory banks and our set of priorities and values, which somehow run through our entire decision making. Sometimes we call this latter part our conscience, sometimes our guidance, sometimes our driving force. As I drew up this list in my mind I came across a few items that I wanted to add, compelled by the result of my recent thought process, potentially contributing factors, of which I had not been consciously aware: instincts and emotions and a certain obstinacy, persistence at whatever it was that I was doing that made me want to go on, continue on the path once entered.

This additional part referred to two opposing forces that did not pull in the same direction. In my own past they certainly had not. While my instincts would have signalled, even shouted warnings, trying to prevent me from galloping off without knowing which way I was heading, obstinacy and persistence had kept me going on regardless, shutting out the forces of reason and – what is worse - my instincts.

This obstinacy and persistence drew their strength from convictions, preconceived solutions to certain scenarios, action patterns that were based on something that may have been instilled deeply inside my personal sphere, my characteristics, the pattern that comes to the fore. Things that happened would trigger off a reaction particular to me. An unknown force was embedded deep down inside me.

Without consciously knowing this I had a number of blueprints ready for the handling of certain situations: like 'doing one's duty and meeting one's commitments and responsibilities', 'the honourable thing to do', 'to care', 'what one does or what is expected of one', whatever name or description it would go by, a set of procedures for the handling of certain given situations. This was most certainly based on a combination of my education, in particular the set of values that I had unthinkingly and without hesitation taken over from my parents and the society in which I grew up.

Where the pursuit of emotional outbursts and pleasures were subdued and suppressed, they escaped into the exhilarating and often spiritually gratifying experience of abiding by the commands of caring and providing on the one hand and honour and integrity as defined by the society in which they lived. These were still the values of Victorian England, even in the Twentieth Century. It was the essence of the austere Christian, particularly Protestant outlook that had placed such enormous energies at the disposal of the British Empire by barring them from brightening up somebody's personal sphere. And I had followed right along in the footsteps of that movement, without ever even thinking that I might have been affected by anything like that.

Come to think of it, what I am describing may be a severe case of crusader syndrome: to resolve problem scenarios by 'doing good', doing good in the sense in which one saw things, one's very own and personal perspective, based on one's own ideas, concerns and convictions. But when this happened it did so at a considerable cost, at the expense of deep, heartfelt honesty, and – worse - at the expense of love! It was a scenario where love had been banned from coming into the equation.

I was shocked when this realisation suddenly broke through into my conscious state of mind. No matter how objective I had always tried to be when thinking about the past and the things I had done, I had always thought that there was a quality of something very good about it, somewhere.

I had been doing good, hadn't I?

Had I, really?

Good to whom, Lydia, Louise, myself?

What is the connection between doing good and loving, is there any? And if you do good, shouldn't that *result* in something good, like making somebody happy? Had I made anybody happy?

Lydia? I am not at all sure: Maybe in a way and up to a point, beyond which disappointment and sadness would have set in.

Louise? No is the only possible answer. We enjoyed the sparkle of moments of innocent youth that were somehow bestowed on us, poured out over us by fate without our own conscious contribution. It had happened because fate had briefly smiled on us. Then we had missed the big opportunity and moved on, going our separate ways.

But at least I would have made myself happy, wouldn't I? That is not even a joke. It is more like a tragedy, someone trying very hard and yet failing so miserably, which – really – was what I had done. I had wanted so much to make someone else and myself happy - together.

That was the key to the whole thing. The first step that I took had been the wrong step. Wrong idea, wrong approach, wrong philosophy and wrong strategy! You cannot make somebody else happy without being happy yourself!

That was it.

All this self-sacrificial preponderance of the right thing to do was no more than a self-gratifying excuse for having denied yourself the freedom that Nature has placed at your feet, for you to take, hold and enjoy, your very own happiness. Even the politicians have seen the pursuit of happiness as one of the essentials of life, although we may in general be a bit short on the follow through.

You cannot make somebody else happy if you are not happy yourself in the process. It does not work! It is against human nature and therefore bound to fail, as it had in my case.

I had entangled myself emotionally with Lydia and had followed it through in a spirit of 'doing good', doing the right or the gentleman's thing, as I had been taught, never pausing to think whether that would provide a stable foundation for the long-term bond between two people, 'for better or worse' and all the other good things that we all know only too well.

Why?

Because I had not learned to love, starting with myself. As much as I adore my parents for the fine people that they were, this is where the trouble started, when they failed to impress upon me that of all feelings and emotions love is the greatest, because it is also the purest. Instead, they had denied its very existence, relating human relations to duty, responsibility and abiding by commonly accepted standards of behaviour. For them as good and solid Protestants the food of love instead of being the essence and fundamental nourishment of life was a diet of sour grapes, to be avoided, if at all possible.

Suddenly I saw the light; I had not learned to love, starting with myself, making me incapable of loving others. Deep down inside all the time I had loved Louise. But I did not allow for this to take effect, because I was not ready to derive my very own personal happiness from this love. Why didn't I grab her, pull her close to me, lock her in my arms and shower her with passion and desire? The desire was certainly there, but I fought it back, subdued it. It would have been selfish.

Really?

That, sadly, is just not true. Love is give and take. You cannot take without giving something in return. But I had not allowed my feelings to take charge. I had not allowed myself to give. I should have loved myself more, then I would have loved Louise so much that I would not have let her go, would not have let her slip away. It was the first step that was the bad one, the self-denial, the inability to break away, then and there, from the confines of a fundamentally joyless outlook on life.

Now I had reached the point where I could see and put together the whole picture. Louise and I had been driven together by the force of love, without realising it. When the situation arose, when I should have held on to her, when all my instincts and inner voices told me that I should have, I had let her slip away, for no good reason, over an accumulation of spur-of-the-moment chicken-shit trivia, that had been allowed to cloud the key issue. We drifted apart and I did not do anything decisive to prevent that.

As I went on in life I felt increasingly alone. My inner self may have known where to find the answer, but I did not listen. Then Lydia, a fine woman of utmost quality and calibre, crossed my path. But I did not love her. I admired her, was awed, impressed and desired her sexually, without ever having established that deep, lasting bond that forms the indispensable prerequisite to a good, solid marriage.

When I thought that I had no other way out I escaped forward, hoping for the best. All the time there had been warnings from my inner self, to stop doing this, before it was too late. I did not listen. Instead, the set patterns of my standards of values and for the conduct of life were used to shut out the instincts and the warning voices.

You can do this for so long, but then you come to the point when it is no longer possible. This is when you risk serious damage to your personality, even to the point of endangering your life, if you persist in going on. At this point the inner self kicks in, steps on the brakes and brings things to a halt. That was when it had made me seek to renew contact with Louise. Had I not done it, who knows, maybe I would have jumped off a cliff. I was ready for that.

My new encounter with Louise was successful, at first. That got a lot of tension out of my system, enabling me to go on without jumping off a cliff or joining the Foreign Legion. I had a second chance. And I let it slip away again, same as the first one and for the same reason. I was still not ready to love, love myself and Louise. Instead I hesitated, trying to 'do good' once again. I managed to address a few problems, but not the key issue: My love for Louise, the love of my life.

Things were allowed to drift along until the window of opportunity was shut forever. From that moment onwards my inner self was on the warpath with my strong and stubborn, outwardly active personality, building up ever so much more tension of penned-up emotions, frustration and sadness.

Until . . . this is the point where I hesitated again and again, unable to go further. There was a conflict that I had tried to shut out of my conscious awareness. Deep down inside there was a clear message of pure feelings, love – but I shut it out of my conscious mind – a forbidden-fruit-scenario, a married woman – someone who might as well be on another planet.

When Yuko crossed my path I was only too eager to throw all my desires in her direction – to shut out the other one. Yuko and I fused instantaneously, without warning or hesitation, unleashing in me a fierce determination to follow it through. That was the moment when my inner self jumped on the barricades again and maybe for the last time. And I allowed for this to happen, surrendered to this option. It had taken me so long to figure out the most fundamental thing in life, but I had figured it out, finally!

From now on I would live by this newly found fundamental truth of life, come what may. My actions prior to and during the flight were now making sense to me. I was driven on, almost consumed, by the desire to see Yuko. I had felt – maybe persuaded myself - that this was my last big chance in life to come out and be unashamedly honest: To love, to take and give love, to surrender myself and take as my own the one whom I had found so suddenly, the one that a kind, forgiving, benevolent fate had steered into the path of the seasoned aviator.

That was what had driven on my inner self. I had not allowed myself any other option. Come what may, regardless, I wanted to be with Yuko; to hell with fuel pumps. I would get there, walk if necessary. That was how things took their turn.

Verdict – Version 3

Subject man underwent a subconscious rearranging of his set of priorities, placing personal happiness at the forefront of his thinking. This made him temporarily unaware of certain aviation related cautionary instincts that could, possibly, have warned him of impending danger. He went on to blatantly disregard his duty to supervise the carrying out of certain tasks that he had delegated to his passenger with the consequence that the aircraft's location was not known to potential rescuers as and when this would have been desirable. It is noted, though, that he in no way neglected his principal duties and obligations as an aviator and the pilot of the aircraft, which he discharged impeccably. Therefore, save for the significant inconvenience of hampering the rescue efforts, the actions taken (by subject man) are exonerated and not found to have been incompatible with aviation safety.

Whichever way you want to look at this, I was still alive and I would use my last remaining breath, if it ever came to that, to be true to myself, henceforth. I desired Yuko, I loved her, I loved myself and I would reward myself with my love for Yuko, come what may, report or no report, FAA, CAA, KGB or whoever else! I had miraculously through all the anguish and excitement of being stranded in the arctic wilderness found my true and fundamental set of values. I was going to set my priorities right, once and for all!

Yes! - It is yes to love, call it longing, desire, or whatever else. Yes, to the very essence of life. But above all has to stand truthfulness. Honesty.

Questions

"If Yuko is your all-and-everything, how come you fantasise over other women? Carla, Shola . . . you name them – quite a harem!"

Harry surprised me with a cup of the most delicious tea. He was a natural born cook and as I was to find out later also the perfect host. He wanted to talk and I gave him an encouraging look.

"Say, old boy, who is Carla?" He said it nonchalantly, in a casual way, with an innocent, friendly expression on his face, perhaps with the hope of baiting me into telling my life's story.

"Where did you get that name?" I was completely taken by surprise. "I can't remember ever telling you about her."

"You talked about her in your sleep; an old flame?" He had put me on the defensive.

"Why old?" I was stalling for time.

"Yeah, right, there's more than one, like Yuko, right?" This increased the pressure.

"I can't believe I talk that much in my sleep!" I was trying to think of how best to avoid telling him anything. "Carla is from way back and Yuko is the one I was going to have lunch with as soon as I got back to Anchorage. She is a friend."

"More than a casual acquaintance, right?" He gave me an inquisitive look.

"Yeah," was all I could reply rather - reluctantly.

"Oriental, right?"

"Why?"

"Well, Yuko isn't exactly a Polish name, is it?"

"Japanese."

"And Carla is Italian?" Harry was increasing the pressure.

"No, Chinese. Harry, stop being such a pain-in-the-neck! You're killing me with your questions. I'm not used to talking about my private life. I've never done that."

"Time you did or you'll turn to stone inside." He was having a wonderful time.

"All right, Harry, Carla is Eurasian, English father, Chinese mother."

"And let's not forget the pretty Chinese mystery woman from the boat! I'd say, man, there is definitely an oriental streak in your love-life!"

"Please, leave her out of this. I don't even know her name."

"Wow, you have a crush on her, I can tell!"

"What makes you say that?"

"Your reaction: emphatic denial, which in plain English is an outright confirmation!"

"Honestly, Harry, stop it."

"So, the silent hero has a sweetheart or maybe two or three? Confess, man!" I was amazed to see how much his mood had begun to sparkle, turning from passive dejection to inquisitive assertiveness, bordering on a mild case of cheerful belligerence.

"My money is on the would-be-fish-food-woman, rescued by Prince Valiant. If you want my view of things she is the front-runner of the pack."

"Say whatever you like, I'll neither confirm nor deny."

"Well, let's face it, if on your own admission you are entertaining Yuko, going out with her and she is your all-and-everything, how come you fantasise over all these other women? Carla, from way back; Shola that you were having a tête-à-tête with just the other night; the mystery woman you saved, you name them! I'd say, old boy, that's quite a harem! Speak, man!"

"Have mercy, Harry." I pleaded with him, but his happy mood won me over. I wasn't going to ruin it by being a spoil-sport and I found myself joining in Harry's laughter. "So, anyway, Carla is from my college days, Yuko I met just recently and Xola – not Shola as you keep saying – is the one with the beautiful dark-brown, actually black eyes, quite black."

"Balls! There ain't no such thing as black eyes, at least not in humans, women to be precise, not to the best of my knowledge. I believe it is a biological impossibility. So we have Carla, thinly disguised as a college pal but obviously still in the running or you wouldn't talk to her in your sleep, Yuko who needs company eating and Shola the black-eyed mystery woman, who is half wolf, half invisible. No wonder you didn't want to take on the skipper's wife on top of all that! Boy-o-boy! If you are running around with all of them you're even more screwed up than I am!" He was laughing out loud and I could also not hold back any more, joining Harry in his sparkling mood. We were releasing the tension that had been building up and this was the first occasion to find us together totally relaxed.

"So who's the lucky one, unless you are a bigamist or even a 'triga'-mist? Wait till the Church finds out about you."

"Harry, if I knew what to say, I would tell you. At the moment I'm trying to figure things out myself. As soon as I've done that you'll be the first to know. It's a promise. I owe you that one after you confided in me."

"Looks like you still got a few balls in the air."

"What do you mean, Harry, I can't follow you."

"Indecision! I think you don't know what to do."

"Oh, but I do! I'm taking Yuko out for lunch."

"In other words, you're going with her."

"Harry, let me off the hook – for now at least. When there's something to tell, I'll tell you, like I said."

"One final thought, before you clam up again, old boy, when you hear that magic voice, telling you it's that one and nobody else, make sure you know which one is talking, the heart or the hormones. When I fell for Sheryl it was the hormones, not the heart. But I didn't want to preach – just tell you what happened to me."

"And it had happened to me with Lydia, let's face it. Now I know it for certain. But that will be enough. Am I excused for now?"

"Shame you're such a chicken, but I'll forgive you this time."

With this profound statement from Harry the conversation was over. I had to admit that Harry's clarity in the way he saw things and told me did reach right into me. He was a brilliant observer.

We settled back into our respective corners and I escaped to my inner world again. I was confused, wanted some breathing space and needed to come to terms with a few things that lay in my past.

I found this brief exchange quite alarming. Without really knowing anything about my situation Harry with seemingly clinical precision had uncovered a serious flaw in my emotional cosmos. Same as Hazel had been competing with the women in Harry's real world, Carla was competing with the woman that I desired, sexually, personally and emotionally, Yuko. But Carla was the product of my imagination. And if that was so she was getting her orders from none other than Jack the aviator, if you wanted to go up the chain of command, something quite natural for a man with my background. That meant me. So there was an element within me that was obviously out to sabotage my potential love-life with Yuko.

And how did Xola fit into the picture? Was she also merely someone that my mind had created or was there a basis in fact behind her and those captivating brown-black eyes of such heartwarming beauty? Even my most vivid imagination could not have invented them. And then, come to think of it, why did my thoughts go back to the sailing adventure in the Irish Sea and the woman I rescued and whose name I did not know?

Carla and Xola were ganging up against innocent, poor little Yuko and the responsible part of my mind immediately rushed to her rescue. Yet, whilst the feeling of attraction to Yuko had been dazzling and overwhelming there was an element of hesitation somewhere. Was Harry right when he – jokingly – referred to me possibly being more screwed up than he; and what about the hormones vs. the heart?

Harry was a big step ahead of me. He had figured himself out, reached what I call his appropriate level of enlightenment, the irreversible power which - once acquired - can never be reversed. I had the right idea about what Hazel's magic had done to Harry. But quite unintentionally I had been a bit pompous about it, thought this could never have happened to me.

There was an inner voice that wanted to reach me but didn't get through. Someone was trying to communicate with me. Suddenly it was there from out of nowhere, the voice of reason, which rang loud and clear: Love is the most beautiful thing on earth but in order for it to ultimately fulfil itself in the successful conduct of the life of those united by it, it has to have a solid foundation. It must be embedded in wisdom.

We like to consider those wise that do not make the same mistake twice, assuming they survived it the first time around. Therefore there has to be a dispassionate and comprehensive assessment and analysis of past mistakes before we give ourselves a chance to blunder again. The fundamental mistake in my relationship with Lydia had been to allow the surge of desire, which culminated in her unconditional surrender. This in turn triggered off my unilateral commitment for ever after, without any means of recourse or correction and recovery.

Instead, we should have allowed our feelings to play themselves out in a mutual and reciprocal acceptance of one another, sharing the joys and pleasure but also the responsibility and caring that goes with it. That process would have allowed us to step back from the relationship if it had come to light that there were elements between us that would be irreconcilable, regardless of time and effort devoted to their solution. That would have been the commonly accepted 'western' way of dealing with the subject. Instead, between Lydia and me the hard truth had been that the first kiss was also considered to be the bond for life. Thereafter her position became that seemingly devoted 'you-decide-Jack', which blocked any potential exit scenario, my escape route if things did not work out. It had been my self-inflicted version of the honey trap.

If I wanted to be the circumspect man who on the professional front is entrusted with the full responsibility for the safe discharge of his duties I had to display the same attitude towards the elemental questions of the future conduct of my life, with or without a chosen one by my side:

The voice of reason had to come into the equation and I had to make sure that Yuko and I agreed on that.

Decision Making Time

"We haven't found them yet." – "Right, here's the plan."

"I've had enough of this shit." It was unusual for Collins to use strong language. "Again we've been sitting on our asses while the boys are out there, freezing their tails off."

"I hope, they're not." Scott Raleigh came walking into the room, waving a map in the air. "I think I know where they are!"

"Man, let's hear it. I can't wait." Bob Masters said what everybody wanted to say. The days of waiting, guessing thinking and not knowing had worn them out.

"Well, first I looked up the weather for the day of the crash or should I say presumed crash and Jack's original flight plan. After their first way point they had a ten-knot crosswind, more or less all the way. Now, look at the magic . . ."

He put his map on the table. "Here is the flight plan, here is the line as reported by Harry and here, starting at the point last reported by Harry and going backwards is the vector denoting the drift due to crosswind since the turn at the way-point. And what does it do?" He had assumed the posture of the math teacher, checking the kids' homework. "Look, it ends more or less right on Jack's flight plan. In other words: Jack was exactly where he wanted to be, Harry just called it in wrong."

"I'll be damned." This was too much for Masters. "The sonofabitch forgot the fucking crosswind."

"But I don't understand. Why didn't Jack listen in on Harry's calls?"

"I can fill you in on that. Jack is a loner, likes to be alone. I reckon he just shut Harry out of his mind completely." For Bob Masters things were now coming together. He looked at Scott Raleigh. "So, where are they?"

"Let's start at their last position as reported by Harry but corrected for crosswind." Scott was having his five minutes of fame and glory. "They carry on straight, no reason to assume otherwise, until . . .' he tapped a pencil on the map. He must have thought that that would give him extra authority, remembering Collins' briefing the other day, accentuated by pencil tapping. "They came down somewhere between this point" – tap of the pencil – "and somewhere before the next fifty miles were up." The pencil, now reversed to write mode, drew a series of oblong, almost elliptical figures that extended over about forty miles or a little more in the real world.

"OK, that's still a stretch of – what – say forty, almost fifty miles." Collins didn't share Scott's euphoria.

"We haven't found them yet." Masters gave Scott Raleigh one of his marine sergeant stares, with which he used to frighten the wits out of young recruits when he was still a drill instructor.

"Right, here's the plan." Collins had turned into mission control once again. "We launch at first light tomorrow morning, regardless of weather. If there is not enough visibility we go IFR. We'll patrol a corridor between the last reported position, as corrected for drift and the fictitious next fifty-mile point, which they obviously didn't reach. We'll use the GPS coordinates of these two as our turning points. We'll fly on instruments at a thousand feet above terrain, northbound, and at seven hundred when we swing around to come back. It's flat there, so it's safe. If the cloud cover breaks we go down on the deck and have a look-see. Otherwise we'll just keep our eyes open. Let's also make sure we continue monitoring the radio. Maybe they were able to salvage a set. You never know. If they did it will be very short range – faint - that is. So, listen up good, lads! At any rate, let's hope for the best. We'll work shifts. Hank and Teresa in the chopper and Scott and Paul in the Otter, you're the first shift. When the Otter comes back for fuel Bob and I do the second shift. We have no second shift for the Huey, so we'll play it by ear. We'll patrol all day, until . . ."

Instant Recognition

Day 6
The wolves . . . Think of all the things that we could do if we had packs!

I have the gift of instant recognition. Some people read, I recognise. Let me explain. The normal reading process runs from left to right, top to bottom, unless you are Arab, Chinese, Japanese or someone from a few hundred other cultures. You figure out the letters, the letters make words, the words have meanings, the meanings merge into idioms and sentences and what you see is a letter from your banker:

"We regret to have to advise you that your account is seriously overdrawn . . . within a matter of days . . . further proceedings in the hands of our solicitors . . . regret . . ."

With me it's different. I pick up a snippet here, a bit there, a little mosaic stone from the middle and with only a small percentage of the total information in my possession I can instantly establish the whole picture, like with this letter. I open it, read the words 'bank', 'overdrawn', 'regret', 'solicitor' and what I instantly recognise is trouble. I do not have to read every rotten little word of it.

The scientists say that is because my subconscious gets direct access to the visual and the visual transmits straight into the recognition centre. That is a bit too high for me and I do not quite buy it. My interpretation is that as a kid I was 'reluctant', that is slow to read and I was observed for hours on end to skip through books, again and again, pausing only to look at the pictures. And with pictures you only need a bit here and there. Pulling from your memory banks you can piece it together from – say – some ten to twenty per cent of picture content. What I saw when I finally managed to make a little hole in the ice on the inside of the tiny cabin window was something worse than trouble. It was big trouble, really huge mega, super-mega trouble.

We had woken up to the fifth morning at our little involuntary holiday home, Day 6 of our adventure in total, only to discover that weather conditions had deteriorated overnight beyond and below what I had thought was possible. I had checked to see how much time we would have before the full force of the blizzard might hit us. What I *did* see were five smudgy dark-white blobs on a background of smudgy dark white, hardly visible in the general mayhem outside and yet presenting sufficient unambiguous information for the instant recogniser: polar or ice bears if you like, scientific designation *ursus albus ferox*, better known as *ursus aquarius*; five of them and getting closer by the minute - fast. I would give it another two to three minutes, maximum, and they would be right on top of us.

Fond as I am of wolves, dogs and possibly even cats, the polar bear stops me cold in my tracks. I treat him with respect and circumspection. Out in the open the word is 'avoid'; you give them a wide berth. If there is a mountain measuring ten miles at its base and they go left, you go right. It's that bad.

In our case there was nowhere to go, because you cannot outrun them. We had no firearms and what protection the cabin would offer was, at best, doubtful. Besides, polar bears have been known to rip apart a little shack like you and I rip apart a traffic ticket that we do not intend to pay. My mind raced frantically, because at the speed of their progress in our general direction time for evasive or counter action was fast running out.

"Put on some weather gear, Harry, we're in trouble, big trouble."

"What's the matter?" He looked at me incredulously.

"Bears, polar bears, five bloody great big rotten stupid sonofabitch polar bears, that's what. They're coming this way and they could be hungry!"

"You're kidding."

"I wished I were."

"Balls! There are no polar bears in this part of the world, we're too far south. Besides, they're supposed to hibernate."

"Hibernate or not, they're for real, see for yourself."

He went to the window, scratched away the ice, looked out and said "can't see a thing. I think you're making this up to scare me."

I did not pay any further attention to him, but scrambled into all of my warm clothes that I could find lying around. Maybe we had to go outside. I did not know why I was doing it, but it seemed the right thing to do. I jumped to the table and had another go at the transmitter, just in case.

In Morse code I tapped 'S-O-S', - 'S-O-S', - 'Q-X', which in our OPS Code Book stands for 'aviators down', followed by the co-ordinates.

As I was about to change the message something suddenly went *Whammmmm! Bangggggg!*

Without any warning, the door came flying into the room, torn away from its hinges, hurtled inwards by an enormous explosive force. The top end came crashing down on the table, smashing the transmitter to bits and narrowly missing my right hand, which I had just pulled away to pick up a pen to jot down something which I wanted to put into Morse. With the whole door a cloud of powdery snow blew into the room, surrounding a whitish, yellowish something that seemed to be attached to the door, still pushing it, until I realised that it was a bear's massive right foot and lower body.

That saved us, at least for the moment.

His bulk or maybe hers was by far too big to fit through the door. Bear cubs are usually accompanied by their mothers, not their fathers, so this was probably the lead female. But I was really not in the least bit interested in working out the specific family situation of our assassins. It does not really matter, does it? To me brutal force is something masculine rather than feminine. That is why regardless of gender issues I like to refer to bears as 'he'. This was an acute survival scenario, not watching a movie on the Discovery Channel.

By putting his foot in first he got as far as moving his body inwards up to below his arms or front legs, rather, when he filled out the frame of the door completely and got stuck. He was roaring and his lower body continued moving forward, expanding like rubber and stretching into the room. We were absolutely terrified. It was the most horrific experience of my life. I cannot think of anything that I had ever experienced before that gave me such an acute feeling of sheer terror, vulnerability and exposure.

We were going to die, eaten by bears.

Then I realised that he could not see us.

Fight back! Don't give up! Do something!

The bear's huge leg was now fully inside the room. The frame of the door was completely filled out by the monster's lower body which - for the moment - had halted in its forward thrust, obviously because the bear had realised that it was not getting any further into the cabin. It looked like a change of tactics was imminent.

If ever there was going to be one this seemed to be the right moment to act. With my bare hands I grabbed the not yet ignited end of a burning log from the stove, totally oblivious to the flames and ember and thrust it against the bear's under-belly. There was a furious outcry of pain, anger, threat and aggression, but my counter-attack worked, at least for the moment. The bear pulled back into the open, until he stood there, about six feet outside the door, glowering at Harry and me. Standing on his hind legs he was towering about ten feet tall, raising himself and stretching his front legs into the air to even intensify the intimidation. If that was what he had in mind, it worked. We were terrified out of our wits. Behind him stood another big bear, maybe last year's cub and three smaller ones.

Our aggressors were perhaps mom and last and this year's kids, but that did not really matter. I could not bring myself to call the smaller ones cubs. They were anything but cuddly toys. I hated them instantaneously and called them 'little monster bears' and the bigger ones front-runners or whoever they were, 'big monster bears'. I have always thought of myself as an animal lover, but – obviously under the terrifying weight of the dramatic circumstances - I am about to make an exception. I did not feel the remotest hint of positive feelings for these bears. Maybe that will change again over time, when I see bears that are not intent on killing and eating me. At this very moment I was a creature in the wild as much as they were – and it was a survival issue!

Had we lived through a plane crash, an explosion and the cold arctic weather to be annihilated by this catastrophe? How were we ever to get out of this, unprotected, face to face with a ruthless enemy? Any second now the big mass of smudgy, whitish fur would once again be propelled in my direction by its occupant, trying to finish me off with the next move. Defensive counter action had now become a matter of desperate urgency, even if only to gain time, time to think and time to act.

"The Very pistol!" I yelled to Harry, who stood behind me. "Grab the pistol and give it to me! It's lying on my bed, with the cartridges. Give them to me, all of it, pistol, ammo the lot . . ."

Well trained sportsman that he was, Harry was alert and on the ball. He opened the breech of the pistol and slid in a cartridge; I grabbed it, pointed it at front-runner-monster and squeezed the trigger. A white flare erupted from the muzzle and drew a scorched black line across front-runner-monster's right forehead, about two inches from the ear, to streak on in a shallow curve until it fell to the ground, splashing into the snow and raising just a little bit of steam from the heat of the flare. It had not caused any real damage, but startled the bear enough to stop him in his tracks again, momentarily. I loaded a second cartridge into the breech and pointed it straight at the bear. As if anticipating another attack from me he dropped onto his four feet the very instant that I squeezed the trigger again so that the flare went right over his head, this time rising straight up on an upward trajectory and carrying on in a shallow downward curve. I had fired upwards from a position lowered on to one knee and the flare streaked harmlessly into the winter sky.

Red.

A red flare, in the aviation world as in international ocean shipping is a danger or distress signal:

"Come and get me!"

"Help!"

I reloaded the pistol to be ready for the next attack. This time I would make sure there was going to be blood in the snow that was not going to be mine. I had now built up the right kind of aggression to want to strangle the bear with my bare hands, if all else failed. The bears had briefly consulted amongst themselves in a huddle like football pros and regrouped to come in for the kill and the meal.

Disgusting thought!

To end our lives as bear food!

Front-runner-monster was obviously getting ready to charge again, this time definitely going to finish us off. One could sense that he was getting increasingly angry and wasn't going to play games any more.

Zzzzoooooooooooooooommmm!!!

As the bear had risen again on his hind legs, so as to be better able to come crashing down on us, a wolf came tearing across from out of nowhere. The bear, startled, turned his head in the direction of the wolf that had passed by at right angles, flying through the air only inches under his nose. The bear lashed out, narrowly missing his target as the wolf may have planned and followed the trajectory of the wolf with the circular swinging movement of his left front foot.

That was a mistake.

While his attention had been absorbed by what had obviously been intended as a diversion, his body still half turned in the direction in which the wolf had continued, half a dozen wolves pounced on the bear simultaneously, having followed closely on the heels of the first attacker. As the bear was still trying to figure out what was going on, each of the six wolves, simultaneously, went for an exposed part of his body, to attack, bite, disengage and run. The cavalry had arrived! The most remarkable cavalry tactics I had ever seen!

As the wolves sped away, I could see small red spots, bite marks, blood, emerging on the smudgy white of the fur, leaving the bear to stare after the attackers in pain, disbelief and with growing fury and anger. But his attention was now divided. He hesitated. His imminent charge in my direction had been halted again, obviously adding to his frustration and anger. The wolf leading the assault had jumped right for the bear's jugular, the others each biting into one of his paws and number six going for the bear's neck from behind, trying to inflict pain and damage, then letting go immediately to make a run for it to avoid the bear's mighty paw.

The bear howled, stopped again, confused, in pain, angrier than before, but obviously not quite knowing what to do next. The other big monster was about ten feet behind him. He or she – did it matter? - had not yet gone into action. It seemed that next-in-line had a dual role, to serve as back-up team and to keep an eye on the kids while there was hostile action on the field.

The initial plan must have been a simple and straightforward one: let front-runner get the food and then we shall all sit down and have a nice little picnic.

No picnic!

The second wave of attack hit the bear, who was just as unprepared for this bolt from the blue as he had been the first time. As he suffered more pain his outstretched left front leg caught one of the retreating wolves just enough to send him somersaulting through the air. Fortunately for the wolves and us he did not inflict any serious damage, as the wolf was able to make a dash out of harm's way. They had raced away to the bear's right, gone around the back of the cabin to reappear on the bear's left while he was still expecting to see them on his right. It occurred to me that our bear was fortunately not very bright; in terms of strategic thinking certainly no match for the pack of wolves and their leader.

Meanwhile two groups of three wolves had each bypassed the principal action and gone straight for two of the kids, this time biting and locking into them to the point where the bears howled in panic, pain and agony. They tried to shake off the wolves and run for cover, each dragging with it the twisting and turning wolves, which hung on to the bears by their teeth. That was enough for mom or whoever was No. two, who turned around to run to the aid of the by now seriously endangered offspring.

The wolves had disengaged but continued to chase the three little monsters, with the back-up-bear in turn chasing them. Front-runner-bear must now have sensed real danger for his companions, and had to make a decision. He also turned around to follow the other big monster and the kids the very same instant that the lead wolf came in for the third attack, this time with devastating and decisive effect.

She was followed by three of her wolves, while one of them, the one who had been hit by the paw of the bear, was holding back, probably in pain. The wolves were moving so fast that some of them seemed to appear in two places at the same time and it was impossible to figure out how many wolves had been involved in the action. They certainly made it look that way. I would stay away from a wolf pack, especially one that is angry, ready for action and means business.

If there had been any lingering doubt in the mind of front-runner-monster, there was now no further question of it. He was running in long strides after his companions and away from these atrocious wolves. One could suspect a sense of angered annoyance, almost panic, as he now had to protect what might be his offspring from totally unexpected and potentially lethal danger. What at first had looked like a casual and relaxed leisure and food procurement activity had turned into a fight for survival, at least for part of his family or team. The prospective picnic now had the makings of a tragedy of human proportions.

At that moment I noticed three things:

The storm had died down somewhat, the cloud cover had begun to tear open in places and I heard an aircraft engine. Almost automatically I fired the Very pistol into the air to release a flare.

Red.

This time it went straight up. I did not wait for things to happen but followed it immediately with our third and last red flare.

Whhhooosh!

The Twin Otter streaked low overhead, only feet above the little mound, my vantage point from which I had explored the horizon the other day.

Rescue! Saved!

The bears were now in open flight, running away fast in long strides, having regrouped, with the kids in front and numbers One and Two providing the rear guard against the pursuers. The wolves were now breaking off the action and as if fading into the background they were gone as quickly as they had appeared to attack the bears. They must have been in a hurry to return to whatever they had been doing and had vanished from sight. My heart went out to them in gratitude: how very nice it would be to have a pack!

We had been saved twice, first by the wolves and now by the people from base. It was only a question of time before the helicopter would be sent out to pick us up. There was no place nearby where one could land a fixed wing aircraft. Therefore the Otter could not pick us up. But that did not matter! They had found us; they knew where we were and they would come and get us. The wolves, whether on purpose or by default, had made sure that there was somebody left to be picked up.

The Twin Otter came around again. I could recognise Collins' red face behind the windshield and his hand waving to us. We waved back and gave the 'all clear' thumbs up sign. Collins buzzed the cabin a third time, this time about three feet above the roof. We all liked buzzing places, flying low over them, a real give-away of every true bush pilot. Then he pulled up sharp and headed off in the direction of the base.

Contact

. . . during Ramadan would disappear into the desert for two weeks, to be alone . . . to heal the soul. A time-honoured wisdom from another culture.

"Bill, I think we've had it. We've got just enough fuel to reach base plus about thirty minutes for comfort - and just in case. We'll do one more run up the road; then we'll head for home." Collins sounded dejected and defeated. He had continued turning the aircraft around until they were again heading in the opposite direction of Jack's flight path, in other words the way he had presumably come. They carried on for another fifteen minutes, during which neither man spoke.

"Hey, listen to this: I think I've got something on the radio." While they were patrolling up and down the search area Bob Masters had been combing through the frequencies to pick up any distress calls or other radio messages, if there were any. He switched the radio signal that he had been receiving through his headphones over to the cockpit loudspeaker, so that Collins could hear it. Among all the static and crackle there was something that sounded faintly like deliberate messages.

It was Morse code! - Only a few seconds' worth of it, then it stopped, before they had time to figure out a meaning and message. But it was clearly from somewhere close by, faint but definitely man-made, a signal.

"I'll be damned if that isn't our lost sons. Shame we could not get a directional fix."

They had listened intently to the crackle from the speaker but there were no more radio signals. When they came to the end of that leg, as per their search pattern, Collins started swinging the aircraft around again, until they were back on the course that would lead them back to base on their final and once more unsuccessful leg of the search pattern. That instant, as the aircraft had steadied itself on the new course, they both saw the red flare, streaking up out of the cloud cover ahead of them, a little off to the right.

No doubt now! Someone down there was alive and in good enough shape to send some kind of radio signals and fire a flare into the sky, obviously after hearing the sound of the aircraft's engine. Then they saw the second flare. At that very instant the cloud cover tore open and there, right in front of them, was the ground, emerging out of the haze and mist. Collins was already adjusting the course of the aircraft, heading for the position where the flares had appeared.

"There they are!" Masters saw them first.

"I'll be damned. And there's a goddam log cabin." Collins pulled up the aircraft to do a go-around. He was overjoyed as he took the aircraft as low as he dared to buzz the roof-top of the little snow-covered cabin and have another look at the boys.

"Yeah, they look to be in fine shape. One more pass and we'll head for home. Time we did too. Fuel's at rock bottom. Let's beat it! Call up base and give them the good news."

Collins had finished the de-briefing and looked around. On the table in front of him was the map.

"So, they're alive and they're right here." Scott Raleigh took the pencil, with which he had been impatiently tapping the table with the rubber-tipped eraser end. This had evolved from habit to compulsion. Collins had started it and now everybody was doing it. It was really a sign of how nervous and on edge everybody was.

"They're in a cosy little holiday cottage. I think that is the total irony." Hank Snyder could not resist the temptation to stir things up a bit. "While we worried our asses off over them, our heroes enjoyed a winter vacation."

"Thank God for that!" Teresa had been under great tension. Her reaction showed just how much the uncertainty had weighed them all down. "Sounds like you'd rather found them frozen solid and dead."

Collins shot an angry look in Hank Snyder's direction. "You know, you really want to watch language like that around here. Anyone of us can wind up in the shit like that. The boys deserve some loyalty."

“What’s the plan? We go now and pull them out?’ Asked Teresa.

“What with?” Collins had reverted to stern-faced mode. “The chopper is no-go until we’ve fixed the damned GPS. A fine moment for it to pack up. Scott, you reckon you’ll get on top of it?”

“Sure, we’ve already started taking out the one in the Otter to put it into the Huey. We’ll need about another hour.”

“By that time it will be dark. They’ll have to hold out another night. But I think they can manage. They looked to be in really fine shape.” Collins breathed a sigh of relief, “we’ll go and pull them out tomorrow morning, if necessary on instruments. We know where they are and at what elevation. That should not be too much of a problem, right?” He looked at Hank Snyder, the helicopter pilot.

“Piece of cake.” Nobody liked the brash chopper pilot, but they all knew that he was a damned good pilot. His skills would come in handy.

I had started straightening up the chaos that front-runner Monster had created.

“Harry, you want to give me a hand with this door?”

“For Pete’s sake, Jack, we’ll be out of here within the hour, why bother?”

“Well, as a nice gesture to the next bunch of suckers that get stranded here, but also for our own good. I reckon we might still be here for at least a couple of hours, until they can scramble a chopper and get it here. Come to think of it, by that time it will be pitch dark. So, we may even be here until tomorrow morning. Yeah, I’d say tomorrow 10:00 a. m. - give or take half an hour. Now that they know we’re safe they won’t go into a flat-spin to bring us home. They’ll do it in the nice, staid company way.”

“Yeah, maybe you’re right. But if they send the Huey they can still pick us up tonight on the GPS. Collins got our position on his; he can radio it back to base and they get cracking. It’s a cinch.”

“That’s not how the company works. They will want to debrief Collins when he gets back to base to make sure they get it right and don't lose another aircraft. Collins will have told them over the radio that we looked to be in perfect shape and can manage another night in a comfortable log cabin. We're not little high school kids. So, let's get the fire going again and have a meal. Besides, I'm dying for a cup of tea. That's what I was going to have anyway, before we were so rudely and savagely interrupted."

"Yeah – sure - no problem. I guess you're right. It doesn't really matter now, does it? They know where we are through Collins."

"Exactly. Besides, on top of the GPS co-ordinates they will also figure out that our cabin is on the map, once they plot the GPS data, I'm quite sure. It appears that it is one of the ones the *Fish and Wildlife* people checked out. Which reminds me: let's make sure that someone from the company comes back out here to replenish the stuff we've used. I want to throw in a bottle of Scotch, stashed away behind the corned beef. That should have been there when we first got here."

"No way," exclaimed Harry, who had changed completely, back into the cheerful young lad that he usually was. "If you leave it in the cottage the bears will drink it. I'd say we ask the company to put one in the Flight-Safety-Kit, to be ready for the crew as and when needed."

"The FAA would have kittens over that."

We both laughed, a happy, liberated laugh, shedding the tension and anxiety. This was the first time we had laughed truly wholeheartedly ever since the crash.

As it turned out I was right. Nobody showed up, it got dark, and things would now go their usual way, as prescribed by force of habit – 'we've always done it that way' - and the company's rules and regulations. They are everywhere. We even have rules for rescuing people. Tomorrow morning, 10:00 a. m., give or take a little, they will be here, sure as hell. I was grateful for another evening out in the wild, especially now that we were out of imminent danger. The bears would not come back. They must have had the shock of their lives. They would not take another chance but will go after food that is not as capricious as we turned out to be; maybe an old seal, if they found one.

"You saw the wolves, Harry, didn't you?"

"Sure thing - couldn't miss 'em."

"Wolves, not dogs, right?"

"Yeah, wolves – lots of wolves."

"Why do you suppose they suddenly showed up, out of thin air, just like that?"

"I haven't the faintest idea. It does seem strange." Harry looked thoughtful. "Maybe they had a score to settle with the bears. Maybe they wanted to chase them out of their territory, who knows."

I was as lost for a suitable explanation as Harry. "My gut feeling is that the two don't get along too well with one another. I once read that wolves treat bears as instant enemies, they go wild when they see a bear inside their territory. At any rate that was lucky for us."

"Sure was! What a bunch of fine creatures!" Harry's eyes shone. "Still, I think this should remain our secret. Let's not tell anybody about this. People will think we've gone nuts."

"You're absolutely right, Harry. It would take too much explaining and overload people's imagination."

Then we both were silent while we cleaned up our little cottage and prepared the meal.

"Are you taking anything home from this?" A little while later Harry surprised me with this question, when he added, "you know, I certainly will. The times when I wasn't saying a lot, I was certainly thinking."

"Join the club." I couldn't have agreed more. "I've been doing my fair share of it."

"Like what?"

"Very simple." I said. "I have come to the conclusion that I simply want to live, stop making my life complicated by asking too many questions. Yeah, I want to live. Just plain bloody live."

"Alone?" Harry looked at me with sincere interest, like a good friend would.

"No." I could not expand that rather cryptic response, but Harry understood.

"Neither do I." Harry looked at me with his nice open face that had regained its college boy innocence. "OK, so I screwed up once and had an unsuccessful relationship. But it was really my own fault. I never should have married Sheryl in the first place. Marrying her was a silly thing to do, especially as I was still longing for Hazel all the time. I reckon I want to do the same thing as you, just plain 'bloody' live – I'm beginning to like your little *Anglicism* - no ifs and buts. Just live."

"Perhaps you might consider a small attitude change." I smiled at him. "Don't get me wrong, I don't want to lecture you, just a thought."

"Lovely, your British understatement. Like what?"

"Pauline. You really roughed her up good and hard. She didn't deserve that. She's a truly fine woman and she has an eye for you."

"I know. I was pretty stupid. Do you think I could patch that up?"

"Climbing Mount McKinley may be child's play compared to that. There is nothing more shut than a door slammed shut by a woman scorned. The champagne is on me if you can work it out."

"It's a deal." He gave me a long, contented and thoughtful smile. "You gonna stay with the Company?" There was more on his mind.

"Actually, I'll give notice. This little adventure has finally helped me to come to the conclusion that I want to go back to something I left a few years ago. First I need to go to East Africa, the country of the Masai. Among other things, Kenya is the country where I was born. I did mention that, didn't I?"

"Sure."

"I need to figure out whether that burning desire to go home has anything to do with visiting the place where I was born and spent my youth. The wolves suddenly reminded me. Maybe I want to live there for a while. I never had the guts or determination to drop everything else and go and do it. Now I know I will. Somewhere in between I've got to fit in doing the kind of flying that I like and sailing my boat."

"Funny you should say that." Harry was all smiles now. "I'll go back east. There's a university in Florida where I can get an MBA in aviation management. I want to get back into a position in business. Let's face it, I'm not a pilot by passion and desire. I don't have that burning ambition to fly, at least not enough to make me into a really good pilot. I do want to go on flying, but just for fun. At the end of the day we'll both remember this adventure in a positive way as having done us a ton of good."

The rebirth of Harry was complete. He was a new man; the thought gave me a deep sense of satisfaction, reminding me of my friend Abdullah in Dubai, who would disappear into the desert for two weeks each year during Ramadan, to be alone.

"To heal the soul," he once told me.

Wasn't that what Harry and I had just been doing, healing our souls? It had taken a demolished aircraft and a string of other events to bring it about. How the wolves figured in it would remain a mystery. I did not make any resolutions, having given up the habit about a dozen New Years ago. But I was going to live! Sure as hell! Like a wolf!

"Say, Jack, I don't want to stick my nose into matters that aren't my business but there's a thing that bugs me: How did a man with your qualifications and background come to wind up flying around in no-man's-land in clapped-out World War II aviation junk? You could easily be the boss of this outfit." This must have been one of the few occasions that he did not call me old boy. Maybe it was because of the nature of what he was talking about. He looked somehow solemn.

"It's not really a big deal and I don't mind you asking. I was a successful aviation consultant. Then I became involved in a very sizeable aircraft deal, a fleet sale with a product support contract attached to it. It took almost a year to set up. Without prior warning the manufacturer shut down, they had run out of steam and were gobbled up by one of their competitors. So the deal could not go through and I was stuck with all my up-front costs. After some soul-searching I decided that I wasn't going to be a risk-taker any longer, at least not for a while. So I sold my business. Eventually and in stages I got to this place. I like what I'm doing. I'm not exactly in love with Karibak but this kind of life suits me very well."

Then the final moment was there. The helicopter had come to take us back to base. It was closing in across the little clearing to the back of the cabin, which the helicopter pilot had selected as his landing site. Three wolves appeared out of nowhere staying at the tree line which surrounded the clearing at some fifty yards from the cabin. As we picked up our few belongings and made our way across to the helicopter they followed us with their eyes, attentively observing every step of ours. This was most amazing and both Harry and I were moved. When the helicopter lifted off with us inside they dived back into the forest from which they had come, leaving us with questions on our minds to which we would never receive answers.

Going Back

It felt good to be with old friends again, even though I had come to say good-bye

"Hey, Jack, old boy." Harry gave me another one of his college boy grins, which had now completely replaced the at times somewhat sullen appearance of earlier days. "Collins wants to see you in the big hangar."

I was off duty today and had come in primarily because I wanted to pick up some books that I had ordered from a friendly bookstore in Anchorage and which had come in by company co-mail; two about wolves, one about the history of the State of Alaska and a Japanese phrase book, just in case.

Collins met me at the hangar door.

"This will be your day, Jack." He was all smiles. "The ayatollahs in Chicago," by which he referred to our corporate head office, "in their infinite wisdom have decreed that your environmental initiative could be good for the company's image."

Shortly after our return from our little involuntary holiday I had been to see Collins about removing the wreck of the Beaver. "You know, Bill, I wouldn't mind doing it in my free time, taking a couple of volunteers and two Weasels and drive across to pick up the debris. I flew along the route yesterday. That's a two-day trip each way, five days in all. I don't think we have the time for that."

"We sure as hell don't." Collins' facial expression had reminded me of an undertaker who is conveying condolences to his customer, the relative of the deceased that picks up the tab.

"Actually," he hesitated for a second; I guess he had an idea. "Why don't you write a memo addressed to me, pointing out that removing the wreck would receive extensive television coverage, showing the company as an environmentally responsible operation. Besides, it doesn't cost a lot to do and it will make us all feel better," he added as an afterthought.

I did not have very high hopes, because in my eyes our company was the epitome of stinginess. That would be the day, if they actually had such a thing as an ecological conscience. But I wrote the memo, suggesting that we could recover the wreck by flying an aircraft out there that was equipped with skis to land in the snow; a short, sharp, one-day operation. We could take a TV camera team along and one of the corporate officers. I suggested that Ingolf Johansson, Senior vice-president Alaskan Operations, could have his five minutes of fame and glory in front of the camera and sing the praises of what a lovely bunch of people we were and how responsible. Of course, I put that into polite company language, which compared to how we talked amongst ourselves was almost a foreign language.

"They're going for it, Jack." Today Collins didn't have that well cultivated, studied funeral director's expression on his face, but showed one of his rare smiles . . . "with flying colours. We're taking the old Three," by this he meant our much loved ex World War II C47, a beefed up military version of the DC-3. "We've already loaded some tools and a couple of winches, wrenches and whatever we need to remove the engine, and fitted skis to the old lady. We'll break down the wreck into small pieces, as much as we can. That way I'm sure we can get most of it into the Three. Harris actually thinks there might be something worth salvaging. Besides, we ought to have a close look at what's left of the fuel pump. That will give the whole exercise a scientific purpose of sorts, to search for the cause of the engine shut-down. So, if you have nothing better to do, I thought you might want to get into some weather kit, boots and snowshoes - you know the score - the works, for playing around in the field. We'll launch in twenty minutes."

"Great," I said. "There's one other thing."

"What's that?"

"Can we take along some basic, durable supplies to restock the cabin, while we're there? We've used up quite a bit of stuff."

"Sure, seems the proper thing to do. Give 'em a list at the purchasing office, to have it rushed to the plane."

"Thanks, Bill." The bottle of Scotch would be on me. I would slip it in behind the supplies when nobody was looking. After all, it could save somebody's life some day or his sanity. And it would be bound to create one hell of a bombshell of a pleasant surprise, because it would be so utterly and totally unexpected by whoever found it.

I was overjoyed. After the initial rejection of my plan I had been attuning myself to a complete loss of face in front of the environmentalists among us, whom I had promised the removal of the wreck. It was bloody decent of Collins to let me fly the Three. After all, the Beaver had been my mission. I needed to finish the job, one way or other. A few days ago I had flown over the site again and found that only about five hundred yards away there was a stretch of unobstructed flat ground or snow covered ice. Once we landed the aircraft we could taxi up close to the wreck, weaving our path around snow mounds and outcrops, with two people marching ahead on foot to check things out and wave the aircraft in, so that we did not have to drag the tools and wreckage all over the place.

After an uneventful flight of about seventy minutes I had the inlet in sight. I went down to about two hundred feet above terrain and flew along the intended landing site, to get a closer look and check for any obstructions along the planned path. I could not see any and took the aircraft around to line up for the approach. As we were coming in to land on the ice and snow covered inlet, I could see a wolf pack at full stretch, tearing across the inlet, kicking up and trailing behind them in their wake a cloud of powdery snow that looked like the vapour trail of a high flying aircraft.

It felt good to be with old friends again, even though I had come to say good-bye.

Reflections

If and when we decide to enter into a relationship with another person it must be for the right reason. A simple truth that takes decades to learn.

After the rescue the company had given us a couple of days off to recover and get ourselves back into shape, including emotionally. I had agreed to stay with the company for another four weeks, while they were looking for my replacement.

Getting back into the 'real world' at first came as a shock. Things that before our adventure would have been 'normal', the proper course of action if not outright important, now looked trivial, unworthy of all the excitement with which we treated them. Yet our energies and attention were almost instantaneously absorbed again by the daily chores, leaving little or no time to think. I had to make an effort not to fall back into the old routine. I was determined not to. My mind had been opened up to a different approach to life and I did not want to lose that again.

With increasing intensity my thoughts went back to the events that had put Harry and me into a snowbound cottage in the Arctic for almost a week. Memories started flowing. First it was just about what had happened to us. Then a broader picture unfolded. It became clear to me that something quite extraordinary had happened. During the days in almost total isolation, save for talking and listening to Harry, I had embarked on a journey of enlightenment that would span the entire range of my understanding of what makes this world with its human inhabitants tick: the human environment, the society we live in, the relationship of the sexes and how we deal with that.

Harry and I were living proof of the fact that you have to put your house in order before you can function properly, as a human being as well as a worthwhile member of our society. Up to that point neither one of us had done that. We had both failed in our relationships with our soul mates, although for different reasons. It was time to get things back on track.

I do not know where you draw the line. But I know one thing for certain. If and when we decide to enter into a relationship with another person it must be for the right reason and there is only one right reason as far as I am concerned: that you both experience a deep, totally unconditional sense of fulfilment and the readiness to surrender yourself wholly, unreservedly and with limitless and unstoppable affection, passion, and desire. If that is the case, I am sure, everything else will fall into place; if it does not you will know how to deal with that, jointly, as a team.

At the first opportunity that I could find I went to see Yuko. She was at work and we only had a few moments while the other girls covered for her and we could sit down in the little office.

"How wonderful to see you again, Jack. I have been so worried." Her face looked tired and drawn and one could tell that she must have been through some days that were difficult for her. "And I have had to think so much," she added, giving me a look that did not hold joy, more like showing a troubled mind.

"Me too, I've had time to do a lot of thinking. Let's get together properly with enough time and a good meal and pick up loose ends." We fixed a date, I rushed back to the airport to catch up with Collins and hitch a ride back to base.

Before I did anything else I had to draw a line under my previous life for good and without having to go back again and again. The time off that the company had allowed us gave me a much needed opportunity to tidy up loose ends. Apart from a number of long overdue other personal items I needed to speak with Harry and get a few things sorted out face to face with him, 'in private' in a manner of speaking and in a relaxed atmosphere. I owed him a lot. He was the one who had got the ball rolling by opening up his inner self, against my initial resistance. Now I was simply grateful to him and quite sorry about the highhandedness with which I had treated him, especially during the early stages of our adventure.

As I soon discovered, Harry was very much the man of the day. Apparently overjoyed at his rebirth and rescue he staged a couple of 'revival events', first at the company and now at his place. His cheerfulness was heart-warming and contagious. Many people at the company besides me suddenly saw Harry in a new light. The true Harry had come to the fore, shifted to one side the big marble plate which had the name *Hazel* carved on it and climbed out, finally a free man. He came up to me with a drinks tray in his hands, all smiles and cheers.

"I'm glad you could make it, old boy. Some of the girls were already crying their eyes out, missing you."

"I'm sure they were." I took a glass of what looked like a vodka-martini from Harry's tray and had a look around his place. Practically the whole company was there, except for maybe one or two who were on duty. The atmosphere was lively to outright boisterous, noisy, with everybody obviously having a good time. Teresa Sullivan drifted over to us with a martini glass in her hand.

"I guess rescuing you guys wasn't a mistake, after all." She gave Harry an affectionate smile and a 'meaningful' glance up and down the full length of his body. ". . . would have been a crying shame to throw such a perfectly good hunk of a man to the wolves."

"Bears," I corrected her. "It was the bears who thought he was just a dish."

"They meant it too." Harry beamed a broad smile at Teresa. "But Mr. Lone Ranger here fought them off with his bare hands!" Having set down the drinks tray he gave me a pat on the back with his left hand, leaving it on my shoulder as a sort of man's hug.

"We were doing great, old boy, weren't we?"

"We sure were." I had also put my free arm on and around his shoulder. We were standing there like two real heroes, bathing in the adulation of the masses.

Having agreed not to mention the rescue by the wolves, as nobody would believe it anyway, we had to be the heroes.

"Listen, hero boy," I said to him. "Fancy a spot of lunch, say tomorrow? There's a couple of things I wanted to talk to you about."

"Well, well, our resident Brit is at it again! That's what I had to put up with the whole week. When I wasn't fighting the bears or the elements I had to listen to him, eat his food and drink his tea. Is there no end?" He beamed at the people around us, adding in my direction. “Sure, old boy. I had almost forgotten what you look like.”

Everybody around us laughed. Then I noticed Pauline, who had suddenly appeared as if from out of thin air and was now standing next to Harry.

“I’m glad you came through, you rotten old bastard,” she said to him with a warm smile and before anybody could say anything further she and Harry were in each other’s arms.

Clearing the Decks

"We, the men, should have known better."
An old fundamental wisdom, disregarded for ages
better known as the 'benefit of hindsight'

I took Harry to a steakhouse in Anchorage to talk things over, not *Sushi Hito.* I would have considered that an act of betrayal, for reasons that had nothing to do with Harry. Nobody in the company knew even remotely about my favourite watering hole. We each had an absolutely delicious, tender prime rib of beef of the kind that you only get in America. Maybe this was yet another way of putting the hardships of our little adventure behind us. We did not really start talking until we were through the main course.

"Harry, I want to apologise to you. I don't think I've always been fair to you."

"Nonsense," Harry blushed a little. Maybe my words had caught him off guard, embarrassed him.

"You know, before the flight I hardly knew you. And then I played the big honcho. I'm not proud of myself." I really meant it exactly the way I said it. It was important for me to get this out in the open, once and for all. "I had no justification for pulling off that Big Daddy number."

"Jack, whatever you did, you did the right thing. You took charge when I was about to let things slip, give up; myself, my life, us, the present, the future. And then you opened my eyes."

"No, Harry, you opened your eyes all by yourself. All I ever did was listen to you." I fumbled around with my wineglass, searching for words. This was not easy for me. "I'm not normally the kind of guy that apologises and says meaningful, heartfelt things to other people. That's because I normally don't talk to anybody. I mean in the sense of sharing things that are vital and dear to us. But you got me to talk, by making me listen to you."

"I'll be damned!" Harry gave me a surprised look. "All the time I thought I was imposing on you."

"Well, rather pompously I thought so too at first. At least that is the attitude with which I confronted you. I was the big, clever old sod and you were the little kiddie."

"Let's face it, that's what it really was." Harry looked at me squarely in a quiet, unhurried man-to-man way and I could see that he meant what he said.

"Maybe it was true, in a way, but only because of two things: I had not yet seen you for the kind of guy you really are, and you had allowed for this to happen. When you started telling me about Hazel I thought at first that this was the typical kind of thing to expect from you. I had you figured out as some kind of loser. What's more and to make matters worse, I saw myself as towering above you in what concerned my competence with regards to relationships and sorting out myself in life, until . . ."

". . . until you started listening to me. Harry smiled, a genuine, friendly smile.

"Yeah, I don't know when exactly the break-through really did happen, but it was sooner rather than later. At first I just felt sorry for you. Like the poor bastard, what a tough situation, you and your love for the myth of the ultimate, forever-gone woman, Hazel."

"Well, let's face it, it was the truth. I had lost myself, my present and my future by clinging to the past." Harry let out a sigh.

For a while we did not speak. There was no need, because we were in complete agreement. Then it was time to set the scales right all the way.

"You see, Harry, you were not the only one. I wasn't exactly stuck or lost in the past, but I was looking back on a failed love relationship as much as you were, what's more one that failed for precisely the same reason: I had embarked on a relationship that was leading to marriage before I had cleared the decks. I mean cleaned up things that lay buried inside me: A deeply rooted love for someone in my past, not realised at the time that finally broke through. That's what had made it impossible for me to love another woman."

"I'll be damned," Harry almost laughed out loud, barely managed to hold back. ". . . you, the always rational and efficient master of life and its little intricacies! Who would have thought of that?"

"Well, Harry, thank God we are all human." I could not prevent a sigh of relief. "Harry, if I really did do anything for you, like you say, here is news for you. You did exactly the same thing for me. Maybe we went about it in different ways, but when we were sitting there in that little cabin, chewing on the corned beef, munching on the stale crackers and drinking that heavenly tea, thanks to you, I had embarked on my own rescue mission, the rescue of my inner self.

"I was an arrogant old sod, thinking of you as poor Harry. The truth is, it was poor Jack just as much. But I didn't really figure that out until I unearthed the whole story: Your whole story and mine. And then I saw where we had both done exactly the same thing, entered into a marriage although deep down inside each of us was with another woman, whether he knew it or not. Because of that our marriages could not possibly work out. You've got to put your full weight behind it, knowingly and unreservedly. You didn't, not because you didn't want to, but because Hazel wouldn't let you, and you didn't have the strength to give her a kick in the butt and tell her to get out of your life. I didn't because I was playing Sir Lancelot. My subconscious inner self had got both feet on the brakes before it was too late, but I overruled it. I had to be the bloody hero, instead of just being plain bloody human and trying to listen to my inner self.

"The result was that each of us married a woman who, ultimately, believed that she had got the whole of the man, but she hadn't. Never mind the little trickery that each of them may have used. That's human and lies in the nature of women. They do that kind of thing without ever having the slightest inkling that they may have employed a little deception. But that is by the by, because a woman has the capacity for loving a man even if she's caught him in her little web. We, the men should have known better. Both of us, each in his way, had done exactly the same thing with the same outcome. That's what I wanted to tell you, because I owe it to you. Without you I would not have been able to figure it out. So, here's to you. Thanks wholeheartedly, pal." I raised my glass towards him.

Harry was touched by my little speech. He also raised his glass. There was an unfamiliar shimmer in his eyes when he said, "You know, Jack, this means a lot to me. The first bit, the listening and the help that was a most neighbourly thing to do. Now, to share your innermost feelings and concerns with me is an honour . . ."

"For crying out loud, Harry! Snap out of it! I can't listen to that glorious American pathos. I'll break into tears in a second. Harry, I have finally come to see you as a friend. Friendship is a two-way street. So it's only normal."

"Well, whatever you say, old boy." Harry had quickly recomposed himself. He was not embarrassed. I think he was moved in the best sense of the word. We were both human, thank God. Then he beamed at me and, mocking what was left of my British accent, he went on: "We, Harry, by the Grace of God, ruler of the dark, dark wilderness, conqueror of the bears, hereby create Thee Sir Jack of Jacks of Wolfland."

With that he wiped his knife on his napkin and tapped it on my shoulder.

"Rise Thee, Sir Jack." He hinted a bow in my direction and with a broad grin on his face he added "and let me pick up the check, you rotten old sonofabitch. It would make me feel real good, old boy."

"Harry, we've been through this before. "I'm just not bloody used to saying nice things to people. I'm touched and, yes, do pick up the check and if you call me 'old boy' one more time, I'll call back the bears!"

"Yes, old boy!"

I had not thought that Harry would ever get that close to me and was immensely pleased that he was still a young lad. He had all the time in the world to sort himself out and get it right as I knew he would, with or without Pauline, or whoever. Harry had been enlightened as to the delicate nature of relationships and would keep the ship in safe channels from now on, by himself and without outside help if need be. Fate is not always bad or blind. There is some good in any setup, no matter how dim and grim it may look at first. Give it a chance!

Things will work out in the end, with a bit of luck and, sometimes, the help of the wolves.

Yuko

"I'm sorry I did not show up for lunch the other day."
The understatement of the century

On my next day off I went to Anchorage for my luncheon date with Yuko, to have a chance to pick up where we had left things, when due to circumstances beyond my control I had to break our previous arrangement. Now this sounded almost a bit like a joke, an ironic one. Yuko had selected a small Italian restaurant, which suited me well. It was a quiet place where one could talk and listen and was not rushed by anxious waitresses or waiters all the time. Yuko looked delightful but I could tell that she was not relaxed, far from it. Her face had concern written all over it. Something was troubling her, something big. I thought it would be a kind approach to help her bring it out into the open, before she choked on it. So I raced through the preliminaries of 'how have you been etc' and steered her to what must have been the main item on her agenda.

"I'm sorry I did not show up for lunch the other day. I had no way of contacting you to let you know what happened."

"Jack, it was quite terrible. First I worried, then I was angry and then I called your company to speak to you. At first they would not tell me anything but then they said that you had crashed and you were missing. Nobody knew where you were." She looked at me with sad and unhappy eyes, where I would have expected to see some expression of joy that I was back. But apparently her mind did not work that way.

"This kind of thing happens in aviation, I'm afraid," I said uneasily. I suddenly did not know what to do.

"Jack, I had given you up for dead. I don't know why, but I thought I would never see you again. And there are so many things we never talked about and things you did not know about me and I did not know about you." There was no change in her mood as she went on, no improvement.

"Aren't you happy I'm back? Come on, cheer up. The world is still turning around and we are still on it. What has changed?" I tried to cheer her up with a warm smile.

"I think something did die: the innocence of our relationship. It became suddenly very serious. Nothing had been discussed and agreed between us."

For a moment I was speechless. It sounded as if she had already made plans, plans that involved the two of us.

So I asked her "like what?"

And then the floodgates opened up wide: "I want to live in America, get my Green Card and find a new position in a small formation, a string trio or quartet, to get back into music. I'm dying without my music and I discovered how much I miss it. You want to get away from America, live on your boat and sail to Africa. What happens to me when you do that?"

I had written her a letter and called her a couple of times before I went to Camp Bravo so that she would know a few things about me. And those things that I had told her had obviously not done an awful lot for her towards seeing a bright and happy future with me.

"Yuko, we may have got a little ahead of ourselves. I mean making serious plans when we have hardly met." I tried to detect a change of mood in her. Not seeing any I went on. "Is this your first time away from Japan?"

She gave me a surprised look. "Why, does that matter?"

"Maybe. I think there is a difference in customs and habits between Japan and what we call The West, mainly Europe and America, where the relationship between women and men is less formal and the role of the woman more independent."

"Yes, more superficial," she said. "In the West the men play with the women."

"If you will, either one plays with the other. It is not playing with toys, more like playing things out until each knows of the other where they stand. It's only then that you can start making plans and decisions." I saw that her expression became more decisive. She was beginning to get into a fighting mood.

"So you were not serious about us. You just wanted to play with me."

"Yuko, stop acting like a little kiddie. We are both grown-ups. We each have to live our own lives and accept the responsibility for what we do. And with a new partnership it is a responsibility for both of them. Both have to do their own part until they are both convinced that something is growing together into a solid future for both of them together or each of them separately."

This went on back and forth for a while, not really taking us anywhere. Then we both got tired of it and I tried to smooth things down.

"Yuko, I cannot remember what this argument was all about. Would you be happier if I had never come back, lost in the Arctic wilderness?"

"You are being mean." There were no smiles to be had from her.

"Isn't it perhaps something else? We rushed off emotionally into a relationship. But so far we have done absolutely nothing, just looked at each other, talked and thought about each other. You know what people mean when they say to shoot sparrows with a cannon?"

"No!" She said defiantly.

"Or making a mountain out of a molehill?"

"No!" More defiantly than before.

"Or throwing out the baby with the bath water?"

"No! No! You are making fun of me."

"No, Yuko, I am trying to help you to understand that sometimes we may overreact to things. First you were upset about my not showing up for a date, then for not knowing, then because I had vanished and then for feeling relief that things had become easier for you, as I would have made it very hard for you to live out your plans."

"Why do you say that?" To my surprise she was not visibly upset about what I had said.

"Well, Yuko, you know that I've been married before - to an oriental woman, different part of Orient but similar attitudes. And that marriage did not work out because we were never on the same level. In the West language is used as a means to explore, find out, discuss. In the Orient language is used to make closing final statements that are ready for being printed. There is no provision in your culture for coming together by exploring things, one about and with the other, before you decide anything."

There was a long pause. Then, to my utter surprise, she said "I feel guilty about this, but to be honest, I have been thinking just that. That I was jumping head first without knowing into what."

"Now you are beginning to make sense." I was relieved that she had said it.

Then, suddenly and without any warning her first smile appeared. "You are not upset about what I said?"

"No, on the contrary. Thanks for that lovely smile." And then we both had to laugh.

"You are not angry with me?"

"No, not in the least. You are beginning to act like a grown-up woman. If you are concerned about my happiness you have to assure your own happiness first and see if your happiness can be reconciled with mine. If not – the whole thing won't work, no matter how hard we try."

"But that would be selfish, wouldn't it, if I think about myself first?" She looked worried again.

"No, selfish is something different. What I said to you is being mature, acting in a way that will help preventing bad surprises later."

"And what about love?" Now she looked right into me the same way she had done on our first serious exchange.

"Love always finds a way," I said with great relief, sensing that the crisis was beginning to resolve itself. "If we are meant to get together, we will."

"Thank you, Jack. That makes me very happy." She moved over to me and gave me a big smile and a hug.

The crisis was over.

A week later we met again. Without any preliminaries she burst out: "Jack, I've had a letter from the Juilliard School in New York, accepting me for Master Class. You know, they auditioned me back in Japan, that's why I came to America, hoping they would take me."

"Yuko, that is absolutely wonderful!" I was overjoyed, for this meant that regardless of what else happened she would have a life of her own.

"So you think I should go?" She looked worried again.

"Of course you go! You are a musician. This is your perfect chance. Take it! It won't get any better. With that under your belt you will find it much easier on the career path."

"Why my belt? I don't wear belts." She didn't know what to make of my remark.

"It's a figure of speech." Then we both laughed, a joyful laugh, for there had just been some truly good news.

"So when do you have to go?"

She hesitated. "Next week," she finally said, worried again.

"Don't worry." I tried to sound as nonchalant as I could. "I'll stop by on my way to Europe."

"Oh yes, do that." Now it was clearly visible that the joy over the good news had overridden all else. Yuko was on her way, her own way. And I was happy and relieved that she was.

I took her to the airport to see her off on the flight to New York.

"Will you miss me?" She asked.

"Yes, lots."

"Will you write to me?"

"As much as I can." I didn't want to make any false promises. "We live in the age of modern air travel. If we want to get together, we'll find a way."

"What will you do, Jack?" We were holding hands, looking at each other with the premonition that this would be for the last time.

"I've been doing some thinking. Same as you with your music I can't live without flying. I've saved up a little money over the years. I'll go to Europe and look for a small air charter or air taxi operation in which I can invest and take an active part."

Then we fell silent – one long tender embrace and she was gone, through the departure gate, to New York and to a new life, the life of a talented and gifted musician that was going to go somewhere – alas, without me.

For the first time in my life my love for a woman fulfilled itself in the same way as that of the woman for me. It was deep, heartfelt love between Yuko and me, which fulfilled itself in our parting of the ways, as there was no other route open through which it could have done so.

It was sad and it was pure.

It was love.

Wolfland

If societies are judged by their systems of order, justice, land rights, and family, the kingdom of the wolf is one of the most sophisticated. Few creatures, two-legged or four, honor a hierarchical system with such respect, teach and nurture their young with such diligence, defend their territories with such passion, and hunt and fight for survival with such dogged ferocity.
Editors, Alaska Magazine, May 1991

Having had to say good-bye to Yuko was not as straightforward as I would have thought. The two familiar opposing forces of old times were there again, one saying

'It wouldn't have worked no matter how hard you tried – so be grateful that it was settled amicably and with dignity, say a little prayer and face the future calmly and without the encumbrance of a failed relationship'.

The other side didn't go along with that at all: 'You never gave that tender blossom a fair chance that it could have taken hold of you and grown into something truly beautiful, deeply rooted and lasting'.

I queried my motives but I had been sincere with Yuko, of that I had no doubt. Remembering Harry's words about the heart vs. the hormones I knew that between Yuko and me there had been no conflict of the two. Perhaps there are limitations as to how well a man can reconcile them. Women are more generously endowed by Nature. They carry in them the beautiful gift of doing so forever, without strings attached or a time limit – if they want to.

For the next few days neither one of the two scenarios clearly gained the upper hand. Then something happened that settled things, once and for all. It was Saturday night. I had been to the Aviators' Den with some of the other pilots for a couple of double scotches, talking shop and kicking the ball around about this, that and the other. When Hector Martinez, one of our new pilots, dropped me off at my place I was in a very good mood and went straight to bed, looking forward to a good night's sleep. I had the Sunday off, not a care in the world and absolutely no problem falling asleep.

All of a sudden she was there: Xola, the wolf eyes, looking at me affectionately, out of the black of the night – just the eyes, the face remaining in the dark, invisible – as always. The eyes were unmistakably those of Xola.

Xola who? Wolf, woman, angel from heaven?

Wide awake, I got out of bed again and poured myself a drink to support a much-needed thinking process. I was as clear in the head as I ever had been, wide awake and alert. This was a signal; somebody was trying to reach me with a distinct message, consisting of one word: Xola.

The message was as unambiguous as I could have asked for. It said that someone called Xola, obviously a woman, not a wolf, had found her way into the depths of my inner self, the most secluded spot in all of what constituted my physical existence.

It hit me with a bang. There was a Xola somewhere, out there who loved me, who had found the way into my heart and I had let her in! This was no more and no less than an unsolicited amorous invasion, like intruders sneaking into a fortress through a secret passage that someone had left open.

Such complicated thoughts pointed towards the fact that I was completely lost for an explanation. The analytical thinker got to work and on the strength of this activity I was suddenly and unexpectedly rewarded with the kind of breakthrough that is usually reserved for the eminent scientists in our midst: I made a profound discovery. An insight emerged that extended all the way to my younger years. It was a simple pattern, one that made sense and now explained a lot of things. The sequence ran like this:

Louise was my first love. She had my undivided attention, affection and did not have to compete with anybody. Chances are we would have become a happy pair forever after if we had both embraced it as our destiny. Then we became the victims of circumstances: The separation, my immaturity and the fact that I didn't have a living soul on earth to guide and reassure me.

So we parted ways and this became *the slowly growing love not realised* that subsequently was to haunt me. Things did not stop there. The unrealised love stayed, lingered and occupied valuable space that should have been available to another woman, my woman, my own ultimate woman, now that Louise was no longer a realistic option.

When I met Lydia two forces were scrambling for the high ground, trying to keep or chase her away, opposing her: *The slowly growing love not realised* that was lounging in the pole position of my subconscious inner self and my equally subconsciously growing lack of preparedness to accept Lydia the way she was. So this relationship became a non-starter, never had an honest chance.

When later on the spur of the moment and with an overflowing heart I rushed to Louise, full of longing and desire, the situation had changed. The *slowly growing love* had abandoned all hope, given in to the sadness of reality and followed the path of expediency. Neither Louise nor I put in a sufficiently determined effort to finally come together with the other. Louise may have been going through a similar experience.

The pole position in my subconscious inner self had been taken over by another woman: Carla Cheung! Unbelievable as that may sound it made sense to the analytical thinker in me. Although a creature of the mind, Carla had been inserted by my guardian angel to keep me out of trouble. By then I had a pretty bad track record in my own estimation concerning good judgment and what I would call 'emotional reliability'.

If I wanted to apply the wisdom with which Harry had enlightened me, the question of heart vs. hormones, experience showed that in some cases I would have difficulty, telling the two apart. And that is putting it mildly, pointing towards a deficiency in my emotional equipment: I did not possess that ice cold rational power of perception when it comes to first-class, high-carat dazzling women.

Nature had provided me with failsafe protection against what Lydia called 'bad women'. It was the 'good women' that would be my undoing, not being able to figure out how good they really were in respect of whatever ultimately matters. Both Louise and Lydia were top-of-the-range superbly fine women, not just by my judgment, but neither one was right for me. I would now include Louise in that summary statement.

It wasn't just me that failed to hold things together when it mattered most. Louise had moved on. That is why my guardian angel had mobilised Carla, the ultimate woman, to protect me against any other undeserving ones that might be waiting in the wings. It had worked, albeit with the small inconvenience that I had remained very much alone. I had become immune to all women that would not reach up to Carla. That meant effectively *all* women! Maybe I was destined to end my days in solitude.

As my last day of working for Karibak drew near, loose ends and unfinished business had to be taken care of and I squeezed my shortening list into diminishing time available. In a sense the things-to-do list was easier to dispense with than the emotional side. Now that I was about to leave, I realised how much living in Wolfland had grown on me, had become a reality that had developed its own dynamism.

Harry, the down-to-earth realist, had a crystal-clear understanding of where we were and what was going on around us, despite his own emotional problems. That had enabled him to throw out any allusions to magic, super-natural and unexplained phenomena: we were two people having lost their aircraft, sitting it out in a miraculously found ex-fur trappers' cabin, waiting for rescue. That was all. The Wolfland idea was strictly mine, something that would have flowed out of my complex personality, my attitude to life and the rest of the world.

More than many - if not most - other people I was ready to accept the existence of things that are a little bit beyond our reach. If they completely lose contact with reality you call such people dreamers, if they excel to new heights they go down as visionaries. History will decide where I get slotted in. It won't be under *having-lost-their-way-dreamers* and probably not under *having-made-earth-shattering-discoveries-savants*.

It is a fact that I would be unhappy if I did not see the far-away horizon often enough. So I was probably not a visionary but a man of vision, or maybe visions. One such vision had become the idea that Wolfland was a special place. As long as they didn't take away my pilot's license I would go through the rest of my days with the firm belief that this would remain so. I probably wouldn't tell anybody about it, but it would be there in the back of my head.

All the time we are confronted with the question of fact or fiction? Does it matter? Shouldn't we perhaps be forgiven for every now and then venturing into the realm of fantasy? Wolfland is something that could exist and if it did would go a long way towards bringing out a few traits that are peculiar to the wolves and their magnificent world.

Wolf and man have far more in common than is generally acknowledged. The fundamental difference is the fact that the wolf has solved the one problem that man ever since his arrival on Earth has not: the successful relationship of the sexes, living together in the wolf pack, in peace and harmony and with dignity and style. If any lessons were to be learned from our little disaster, at least for me personally, it was to be this fundamental realisation. It may not have been that obvious to me then and there, but it did eventually filter through as something quite definitive, after I had had more than ample time to turn those remarkable events over in my mind.

I thought about what kind of shape I was in following our little disaster, the unscheduled landing in the rough. When you have just been through something like that, are cold, hungry and feel generally miserable you may be forgiven for allowing your thoughts to wander, immersing themselves in the vibes that emanate from the surroundings.

Of course, there had been no talking wolves. I had to agree with Harry on that. The mere thought was absurd. The logical conclusion was that my mind had produced a scenario that under the circumstances I had been only too pleased to accept as reality.

There were a number of other issues, like whether the company would be tempted to go for the insurance instead of looking for and saving us. Some people in management would have had no problem with that. I was relieved that this aspect had not been put to the test. You never know.

The environmental aspect concerning the wreck had been a very important point for me. I was glad and grateful that we had been able to resolve it satisfactorily when we went to salvage and bring back what was left of the Beaver. It is good to know that we are becoming more and more consciously aware of the fact that our

Earth is a place worth saving. After all, to the best of my knowledge it is the only one we've got.

Then there was the question of how much sense it made to plunder the Alaskan resources so that we can all get enough gasoline to drive to the post office next door instead of walking the fifty or so yards. But that was politics, economics and a lot of other things and totally beyond my reach.

I had no problem with the question of whether or not the wolves had in any way helped us in finding the cabin. Contrary to common belief wolf and man are not instant enemies. The human species is not part of a wolf's diet and it requires unusual circumstances for a chance encounter to result in a hostile confrontation. Usually, if left in peace, wolves will avoid contact with humans altogether.

There is a lot of historic information available where wolves have shown behaviour towards man that is more commonly associated with that of dogs, maybe something genetic that could under certain circumstances create a bond or kinship. There are many accounts of cases where wolves adopted and raised human infants that they found abandoned. For me it would be credible that a wolf pack resident in that particular stretch of land would have a memory of previous visits by humans who used the cabin for shelter or even lived there.

I have no personal experience of any kind gestures that were extended to humans by wolves but I have seen ample proof that animals can have feelings and emotions and can show social concern. I remember one special occasion at a watering hole in Tanzania: An elephant was so outraged about a crocodile that wanted to drag an antelope into the water that it gave the crocodile a kick in the butt, which made it somersault through the air. It had to release its prey, permitting it to scramble to safety. So for me a little bit of help and guidance from the wolves would be credible. Maybe the previous occupants of the cabin were particularly friendly with them. Perhaps they gave them food on occasion, who knows?

Should we really draw hard and clear-cut lines of demarcation between what is, what should and what could be? Life holds a lot of mysteries. I like to believe that out there in that cabin Nature saw fit to make me privy to some of Her remaining great mysterious secrets. After all, there is a large enough crowd on earth that demands of you that you should believe all sorts of things without offering any credible proof. So shouldn't we be free to believe something here and there that eludes others? How much do we really know about life? Here we had been caught up in our various everyday challenges, entangled in partnership and job problems with little to no guidance and no helping hand to reach out for us.

Theoretically both Harry and I should have been able to undergo the same identical realisations while being exposed to the same outwardly perceivable circumstances. But any two people cooped up in the same room already go through a totally different experience that will reflect the state and condition of their personality and the effects of their past and previous life, their fears and expectations.

As for Harry and me we would probably have agreed on what we tell our banker and the FAA but above and beyond that we would each of us have connected with his own little world that we cannot share with the other but which is real to the one experiencing it. As far as I am concerned the wolves around us that night had been real. I am prepared to swear to that.

That still left two questions to which I needed answers: From where had I got that name Xola, just like so, out of thin air, without any warning? Who is Xola? I was absolutely certain that I had never met anybody of that name and that there was no Xola with whom I had ever come into contact.

The other question was whose beautiful dark-brown-black eyes I had been looking into and how they related to Xola. Much as the mind may be capable of inventing imaginary things there needed to be a factual basis behind whatever images it produced. The mind can project the idea of looking into somebody's eyes. But these had been very specific eyes – and they belonged to somebody, to a mysterious Xola.

Was there perhaps a confusion of names or identities? They were not Yuko's - and I could not think of any other woman to match what I had seen.

. . . really, is that the truth?

Wasn't it time to face facts?

There was a thought that would not go away. What if . . . ? Shouldn't I put in a determined effort to find out? I could do that on the way to Europe! I needed to find her and get this matter out into the open! I was longing to find her, burning with desire to find her, the one whose name I did not know, the one whom I had tried so hard to forget for fear that I could not cope with things when I saw her.

Is that Xola?

If the eyes I keep looking into belong to the one that I am more and more convinced it is, Xola has to be the name of my mystery woman . . .

Do I still have to deal with the *Xola wolf* question? Just to get this settled, once and for all, I did not look into a wolf's eyes that night when we more stumbled and fell than marched towards the cabin. It was dark and I am quite sure that I did not get close enough to any wolf to be able to make out such detail with any degree of certainty. Whatever I saw had been produced by my mind. Somewhere there remained an unresolved element of mystery, an unknown force that communicated wit me.

I needed to find out.

Not find out whose eyes they were. I knew that, had known it all along, just tried to ban it from my thoughts. This wasn't about seeing eyes. I kept looking into eyes that wanted to tell me something and it was time I found out what and face up to it! And that's the next item on my to-do list, find her and find out - look into those beautiful eyes - again - for real.

Trying to draw a line under what happened, I find myself on the edge of the unexplained, where an element of fantasy may have crept into the memories. Maybe I had not only allowed but invited it to become part of that which I choose to remember of our adventure. Until only a few centuries ago it could have cost you your life if you did not believe the Earth was flat and now every child knows it's not.

There exists a sliding boundary between that which we believe and that which we know. This boundary is steadily on the move towards expanding the range of our enlightenment and the knowledge in our possession. So be prepared that some day that which you may find hard to believe today will at some time in the future have become recorded history.

Epilogue - Flying Home

"Thank you, Jack, thank you for saving my life,"
said the beautiful-brown-black eyes

The next two weeks brought an exceptionally heavy workload as in addition to my normal chores; I was tidying up loose ends and briefing my successor. I had practically no time to think about anything – and was grateful for it.

My last day of flying for the company came up with one final flight, ferrying a DC-3 from base to Camp Bravo. The aircraft was to be stationed there in compliance with a new policy to decentralise that one of the wizards at headquarters in Chicago had thought up. It was not a true ferry flight, as that would have meant no payload. On the contrary, the aircraft was particularly heavy, having been stacked to the hilt with spares, tools and equipment. When I queried this, Collins suggested that this was probably some accountancy trick, as otherwise one part of the company would have had to bill the other for operational revenue. Be that as it may, I was sufficiently s-a-t, which stands for sick-and-tired, of some of the corporate trickery and skulduggery and I had only one desire: to get away from it all - fast.

At 10:40 a. m. local time it was chocks-away and a couple of minutes later I was taxiing to the eastern end of the runway for takeoff. They had given me a young co-pilot with practically no flying experience and I made a special note of keeping a close eye on him, so as not to repeat that old mistake.

The airport at base was listed as a Private Airport, which meant that it did not have what we call an official FAA-Tower, where ATC would be government business. Instead we were free to run it as we pleased, within certain limits, and ATC was handled intermittently only when there was traffic that we were expecting or dispatching. Today it was Collins' turn on the Tower. He probably made sure he got it as his way of paying me his respects, giving me the send-off.

"I see you drew the lucky number, Bill." I called him up on the Tower frequency. At a public airport such loose talk would be tantamount to a crime: No private talk on ATC frequencies! But here it was a bit like giving a rock concert in your own garage; nobody cared.

"It's a shame you're going, Jack, you old son-of-a-gun. It was good to have you here." That would have to go down in aviation history as an emotional outburst, coming from Bill Collins. "Take care of yourself and stay out of trouble."

"Yeah, Bill, I'll miss you too. Shame you're not a pretty woman! I almost like you, you old bastard."

"Look who's talking." Collins sounded as if he had a lump in his throat. He was one of the people at the company that I cared about.

"OK, Bill, let's get it over with. Put the knife into me, tell me to shove off." I thought we might both start crying if we didn't somehow snap out of it and broke away.

"Oh – hold it, Jack, I'm just getting a hand-over from en-route ATC. There's a Cessna Citation heading our way. They should call me in a tick on our tower frequency, so cut out the dirty talk while they can hear you and hold until after they've landed."

"Got you, Bill, I'll pull myself together." We had to revert to what is known as 'appropriate behaviour'. This casual atmosphere was what I liked about our kind of aviation out in the bush. We enjoyed an enormous freedom, as long as we were *entre nous*, in a manner of speaking.

An instant later the Cessna had switched to our tower frequency, on which I was listening in, waiting for departure clearance.

"*Karibak Base Approach Control*, this is Cessna Citation Golf-Zulu, requesting permission to land." A woman's voice! I'll be damned, not merely a woman's voice, a British woman's voice that I had heard before. I'm good with voices, don't easily forget them, especially the good ones.

"*Cessna Golf-Zulu. This is Karibak Approach Control, being Karibak Tower:* You're cleared to Runway 27. Zero head or crosswind. No ice or snow on runway. After landing turn left on Taxiway Delta and proceed to in front of the big hangar. We'll send a car to pick you up."

"*Karibak Tower – Citation Golf-Zulu*, I roger that." Her call was too short and businesslike to help me in trying to put a face to that voice. Must be someone I met when I used to go to the UK a lot.

"*N24KP – Karibak Tower*, you're cleared for departure after the Cessna has passed; God speed and *bonne route*." Bill Collins was fluent in French, having gone to school at Mons Air Base in Belgium, when his father had been stationed there under a NATO assignment. He liked to throw in the odd bit of French when he talked to me, thinking that it would make me feel good. This was his and the company's official farewell, which I acknowledged formally, for the record, taxied onto the runway as soon as the beautiful all-white Citation had floated past me and took off for Camp Bravo.

"What was that all about?" asked my young co-pilot, now speaking up for the first time.

"Bill Collins and I go back a long way. That was his good-bye."

I set course for the marker beacon that stood fifty miles due south of Camp Bravo. The young lad had asked me to let him fly but I had declined, which on other occasions I would not have done. This was different, my last flight for the company, perhaps also my last flight in a DC-3. I wanted to have that special feeling once more and I wanted privacy.

"Say, I didn't even catch your name, funny as this may sound with you being my co-pilot. They never told me."

"Peter." He smiled as he looked my way. "Peter Spalding."

"Nice to meet you, Peter, this is my last flight with Karibak. You don't mind if I'm a bit nostalgic and not talk, do you?"

"No, skipper, works fine for me."

"I haven't been called skipper for a long time. You're a Californian, aren't you?" I looked his way and grinned. I had lived in California too long not to notice.

He grinned back. "I guess it's obvious, is it?"

"Yeah, sometimes it is. It's that beach-boy cheerfulness, even if there is no excuse for it." We both laughed and then fell silent until it was time to call up Camp Bravo and let them know we were inbound. I had made the turn to the left at the beacon and was running straight-in in the direction of the runway. Unlike base Camp Bravo had no Tower worth speaking of, just a shack adjacent to the main hangar with a radio, monitoring equipment for weather data and a remotely operated radar. Here landing was routine, most of the time. Every now and then there was the odd bit of local traffic, a chopper departing or coming back from a rig, hardly ever more than that.

"Camp Bravo, this is N24KP, good day, request landing clearance." This was very informal, but at the other end was the office manager, not an aviation man at all, just someone keeping an eye on things. I didn't even try to make it sound formal.

"Good Day from Camp Bravo to N24KP.

"How nice to hear your voice once again, Jack, there is traffic ahead of you descending from 30,000 foot. But there's no chance you running into them from behind. It's a jet, but keep your eyes open, anyway." He sounded excited. I could not remember that any jet had ever landed at Camp Bravo. This must be a very small jet.

When we were a little more than a mile and a bit from the runway threshold we could see it in the bright and beautiful sunshine, perhaps the first good weather for ages: A Cessna Citation; must be *the* Cessna Citation, just landing.

Two minutes later it was our turn to touch down as the Citation had already cleared the runway and taxied to the general aircraft parking area in front of the camp's big hangar. As we rolled up to park next to the Citation on its left I could read the aircraft's registration number: G-ZULU. So it was the same Cessna, British registration. When she had said Golf-Zulu I had not quite known what to make of it, for it did not sound like a complete registration number, taking 'Zulu' for meaning the letter Z, so the registration would have been 'GZ', but now that made sense. I was bursting with curiosity who would come out of that Cessna, so I had taxied up close enough for good wingtip clearance but not giving much away. My young co-pilot was awed.

"Wow!" Was all he said.

"Clean up the store, then go to the office next to the big hangar and do the paperwork. I'll pop across to our British friends to say hello. You'll probably find me in the cafeteria hut afterwards." He was happy that I finally gave him a good enough reason for being there.

I turned back through the cockpit door into the cargo compartment, went down the slope through the passageway and out of the main door on the left. Somebody had already opened it from outside and pulled up the steps in front of it. As I ducked under the nose of the *DC-3* that rose high into the air, to shorten my way to the other side, the captain of the Citation was just stepping down onto the tarmac, smart dark-blue uniform, four stripes and all, an all-weather parka draped stylishly over it and her shoulders.

A woman! The one who had called ATC was obviously the captain, a woman and what a woman!

And then there followed the hammer-blow. As she turned towards me and got closer I looked right into her eyes: Brown-black eyes, wolf eyes, beautiful-brown-black-Xola-wolf-eyes, looking at me out of a lovely face with an oriental touch that I had tried so hard to refuse to remember and yet had been unable to forget. I was speechless, thought my knees would go weak.

"Hi, I'm Zola Bennett, nice to see you again, Jack Donaghue." She had come closer.

". . . the black eyes that I've been seeing in my dreams!" I finally burst out, having at first just stared at her - shaken. ". . . the brown-black eyes of Xola, the wolf, in a captain's uniform. Hit me to make sure I'm not dreaming this."

She gave me a beautiful, warm smile, amused at my obvious confusion. "You're not putting two and two together, are you?" She asked with yet increased warmth, even affection, in her eyes and in her smile - smiling eyes. "What's with the wolf?"

"Last time those very same beautiful brown-black eyes looked at me was on a dark, snowy night after we had crash-landed a DeHavilland Beaver about halfway between here and our Base and were surrounded by shadows which looked like a wolf pack."

"And you just said that wolf had a name? Did you say Zola?"

"Yeah, Xola," . . . unaware that the pronunciation is the same in the English language.

"I guess you didn't catch my name just now. I'm Zola Bennett." Now she knew that I was completely puzzled, temporarily unable to move. Maybe she wanted to tease it out just a little bit longer. "And before they looked at you out of a wolf's head, can you remember seeing them before, on another occasion?"

"Of course, I instantly recognised your face and the voice!" Somehow I had been slow to place the face where it belonged, with the dramatic events on *Swiftcloude.* The ear was quicker than the eye, having found a match in my memory banks for the voice that made an SOS call and the one that asked for clearance to land at Karibak.

"You're the woman from *Swiftcloude*, the wife of the skipper!" I was beginning to function again. "You certainly look different. I was quicker to recognise you by your voice. I am good with voices, I know that!" I just added that to cover my embarrassment, not knowing what to do.

"I'm the woman you saved from certain death in that deckhouse onboard *Swiftcloude*, but not the late skipper's wife. If it hadn't been for you I would have joined my uncle, the skipper, whom you also saved. Unfortunately he did not survive for more than a few days. His internal injuries had been too severe when the mast crashed down on them and he was trying to save the two others."

"I'm sorry to hear that. So he saved their lives?" I was still fumbling around awkwardly, not yet fully connecting with the true meaning of what was unravelling itself here.

"They would have both been killed by the falling mast if he hadn't pushed them out of the way, as I would have been if he hadn't sent me into the deckhouse to call for help, before the whole thing had turned into a genuine SOS situation. And then I was trapped in there." She had come up close to me and suddenly, on impulse, threw her arms around me to lock me into a wonderful, warm embrace, which was only too eagerly reciprocated by my now wide awake and overjoyed body.

"Thank you, Jack, thank you for saving my life," said the brown-black eyes. It was a long embrace that was nourished by more than the impact of the unexpected encounter. The warmth and affection that flowed through it had grown, unnoticed by me, who carried in him, in his subconscious mind, the image of brown-black eyes, connected with the name Xola, wolf or no wolf.

We finally managed to untangle ourselves as practically everybody that was at Camp Bravo at the time was standing around us in a semi-circle, enjoying the unique spectacle. Somebody said "Look at old Jack, making inroads with a veritable four-striper captain, English at that and definitely female." All around us laughed and we had to laugh too.

"My long-lost sister," I announced to voices from the background that shouted 'liar' and 'that'll be the day' and there was more laughter.

When we settled down at a table in the cafeteria hut I noticed that we were still holding hands. "So I looked into your eyes in the deckhouse. But it was really too dark. And how did I get your name. I don't remember, you ever telling me."

"Yes, I did, I shouted it, when I looked down at you as they winched me up into the helicopter in the boson's chair."

"At the time I could not hear or understand a single word. Maybe my subconscious mind picked up what you shouted down in my direction, when you looked me right in the eye. That would explain why I have been seeing those brown-black eyes that told me they belonged to Xola." I was overjoyed – a new-born man. "That leaves one mystery. How do you spell your name?"

"Z-O-L-A"

"I knew it." I exclaimed. "You're a fake. My Xola spells her name X-O-L-A!"

"Just you wait, Jack Donaghue, I'll teach you how to spell my name!" She pulled me even closer to her.

I could not take my eyes off her beautiful face with an oriental touch – a trace of Chinese, I thought. She must have sensed that for the first time and in full possession of my unobstructed powers of observation I was trying to figure out why Zola Bennett had an equally beautiful and slightly Chinese look about her.

"Did you expect Zola to be a blonde, blue-eyed English country girl from Devon or Cornwall?" There was a wicked smile and I sensed with great delight that this woman would be quite a handful. Maybe I had finally in life found my match, an equal partner, definitely not the yes-you-decide-Jack type, rather one that would be my steady rock in the stormy sea just as much as I would be hers and probably give me hell when I needed it. "My mother is Chinese, anything wrong with that?"

"On the contrary, it's great. I love that Colonial touch."

"Don't colonise me!" There was pride radiating from her words.

I had a flash-memory of my fantasy-friend Carla Cheung who had crossed China on foot in the revolution and made it to Hong Kong. Something was coming together here: unknown superior magic in my past implanted this desire-chip in my mind, where it languished unnoticed and unloved until the time was finally right. When I had been ready to go looking for Carla Cheung, Carla Cheung had come looking for me. Zola? Carla? Same woman! Zola *was* Carla! Some incredibly ingenious, divine force had had the grace to create in me a safe haven, where the spirit of Carla would defend the realm until Zola in the flesh was ready to step in and fill it out with heart and soul. My great love of all these many years had finally caught up with me, after I had stopped running away from her, trying to find her.

"Hong Kong?" I asked her with a bit of a smart ass's grin, that of a guy who knows all.

"Yeah, indirectly, my dad caught my mother in a trap in Hong Kong, clubbed her over the head and carried her off to his wigwam, where they lived happily forever after: first Kowloon, then Rangoon, followed by Zanzibar until he finally left the RAF, which had seconded him to the Colonial Service.

Then he started an air taxi operation together with my uncle. My mother was running the whole thing, working the till and keeping an eye on the cash box. I was born somewhere among all that." The best way to describe her facial expression was signalling lovers' belligerence. She was already showing me who was the boss, with an affectionate smile, staking out her turf and I loved every second of it.

"Yeah, that's the spirit. I can't wait to take that just a tiny step further when we can settle this at close quarters."

"Tread cautiously, Jack Donaghue, I'm a Black Belt in karate."

Then she told me how she had started looking for me as soon as she had been in good enough shape to do so. *Uhuru* and I with her had somehow vanished from the face of the earth, which I could clear up from my side. We had slipped into Dublin Harbour just before midnight, unnoticed. At least nobody challenged us and nobody seemed to care, just a trawler putting back into port. We had moored at the shipyard, handed the ship over in the morning and each gone his own way to whatever we wanted to do next. Dublin Harbour Master had been unaware of our presence and nobody asked the shipyard. When enquiries came about *Uhuru* and the ship's skipper, both from the Royal Navy and from Zola, it wasn't until four weeks later as she left the yard to go back to work that the Harbour Master's office spotted her, this time with a hired crew on board that knew nothing of the dramatic events. So it took some more time to finally get my name through the charter company and again more time until my whereabouts finally came into focus. She had used her next available possibility to come and see me, extending a commercial charter from the UK to Minneapolis, Minnesota, to go to Alaska. She thought writing a polite thank-you note would not do, under the circumstances.

"What are your plans, Jack, what will you do?" She asked.

"This happens to be my last day of work for this outfit."

"I know, they told me at Karibak base. That's why I came chasing after you before you could escape me once again. Thank God a Citation can still outrun a DC-3." I looked into a happy face. "So what's your next move?"

"Getting to England ASAP."

"Want a lift?" She gave me another warm smile.

"That would be great. Is that OK with your company? We'll have to agree a fare."

"The ride is on the house. You can sit in the right seat. My Co is already on another job. This model Citation is single-pilot rated for ferry flights. When are you ready to go?"

"As soon as you have finished your coffee," I burst out, "nothing holds me back here and, by the way, I'm typed on the Cessna Citations 1 and 2." Suddenly, aware that I was still holding her hand, I asked her what she was doing in life in general and in aviation in particular with four stripes on her sleeve and a Citation under her fanny.

"I'm the boss of a small charter company. We have three Citations and three Cessna Caravans, that's all. Jack. I don't want to jump the gun, but you being a pilot, my saviour and man-of-mystery have entered my life in a special way. I am in desperate need of help."

"What kind of help? Do I still get to hold your hand if I work for you?" holding on to it as I said it.

"It was my uncle's company and I worked for him as his chief pilot and minority shareholder, representing my dad's estate. It is a very demanding job and you by my side would be a godsend."

"Would I be allowed to buy into your company? I would be uneasy with a free ride. I wasn't going to work for a boss any more, not even one as glamorous as you."

Her eyes shone as I said that. She must have liked what I said.

"Aviation is a tough business and we are practically bust, to be unashamedly honest." She beamed at me happily, as she said it.

"I would have suspected you of being an enormous liar, if you had said differently. If you want to go through with it, so will I. As far as I'm concerned, it's a deal. I think I can scratch together enough loot to buy a reasonable share. And I'll be delighted to work my guts out, if that helps, I mean for you as my boss. I've just changed my mind in that respect. I think I can handle you."

"Wonderful." Her eyes shone.

"Zola, I'd like to make sure we're not confusing issues here. You got under my skin the very first instant when I plucked you out of that half-flooded deckhouse on *Swiftcloude*. But I had you as the skipper's wife – taboo. I've been trying to forget you ever since, trying hard."

"You're still trying to forget me?"

"No, of course not. At the time I thought that it might have put you under pressure if I had come to see you and you being the skipper's wife and on top of that I might have done something stupid."

"Well, now we're here and I'm glad I have finally found you. Maybe having your life saved does something to a woman. I fell in love with you on the spot before logic and reason could have confused the picture. If there is such a thing as love-on-first-sight this is it, as far as I am concerned."

"Strangely enough, the hardest part for me was, not knowing your name."

"But you did! Xola is close enough."

"The Xola name did not break through into my conscious awareness until after our little rough landing. Obviously, you shouted it and I did not consciously pick it up but something inside did and brought it to the fore when fate saw fit to administer a blow to my head, like when I banged it against something."

"Well, thank God for that and I really mean it. Jack, this is not easy for me but I have to say it. No matter how good or bad your excuse, you should have come after me, tried to find me, tried to find out. Do you realise how hard it is for a woman to be rescued and then to be thrown away by her rescuer?" Zola said that with such an affectionate smile that it was quite clear that she was not trying to hurt me, just getting something off her chest, something important.

"In a sense, I reckon that I should have come after you, but my motives for not doing so were pure. Am I forgiven?"

"Of course."

"This may seem a bit late in the day but I was actually going to try and find you on my way to Europe and the UK. I made up my mind about that. I wanted to put an end to the uncertainty as to who you were and what you were doing. More and more I have been thinking about my Mystery Woman – about you and not knowing anything about you."

"I'm glad to hear that, Jack."

"By the way, I did not associate the name Xola with you. When it first got into my head it belonged to a wolf. It may sound a bit silly but I really believed that in some inexplicable way – until recently."

"Well, I think we'll be able to live with this now that we've got it all sorted out. There is one more thing you should know, though, from my end, maybe you'll reconsider your generous offer after that."

"What's that?"

"Part of our operation is at Mount Wilson Aerodrome in Nairobi, Kenya, mostly dedicated to the game-lodges for the tourist traffic, the three Caravans and one Citation." The brown-black eyes had a concerned expression when she said that. I sat up with a start and she added ". . . that's no-go for you, isn't it?"

"Zola, dearest Zola, you don't know what you're saying. I love Kenya, was born there, in Mombasa, to be precise."

"Jack, now that I feel that you might be able to deal with the grave consequences I have to ask you a very, very serious question." Again a little wicked smile appeared on her face. She paused for a moment to size me up. "Do you know that the Masai say that if you save someone's life you physically own that person, I mean hands-on, for keeps, to have and hold, even to take home?"

"Yes, I do, but how come you know it?"

"I was born in Kenya, in the Masai Mara. My parents were the owners of a tourist lodge there and my dad and my uncle built a couple of landing strips and got air-taxi services going after he had worked for the British government. This makes us both fellow Kenyans by birth and British citizens; you even an Ex-Colonial Briton, if I guess correctly. This, of course, also means that I am now your property, Jack, in keeping with our time-honoured tribal traditions. Do you want to own me, Jack?"

"Breaking tribal law would be the most awful crime, wouldn't it? We can't allow that to happen. Zola, you are irrevocably mine, forever. I won't let go of you again."

What a wonderful turn of events. In my life I had gone full circle. I had finally come home, home to Zola.

And then I could see it all quite clearly: being home is not being in any particular location, in a place one can find on the map; being home is having found a safe haven for the soul, the spirit and the heart. It is a state of mind as much as a state of being, being at peace with oneself and the rest of the world. And above all else, being home is being in love, experiencing fulfilment of a man's ultimate quest – no need to look any further. For me, being home is being in the arms of my loving woman.

"Zola, when I was flying that Beaver from Camp Bravo to our base I was actually on the first leg of my trip home, without really knowing where I was going – just searching for home with not much hope – quite honestly – of finding it. Now home has come to me. You have come to me to bring me what I desired and longed for so much and could not find by myself, your love."

Zola hardly ever turned those wonderful brown-black eyes away from me. "What do you say, Jack, shall we get the hell out of here?"

"Yes, Zola."

"Would you like to help me with filing a flight plan, Captain Jack Donaghue," she said in a mocking senior captain's voice.

". . . where to, Captain Boss?"

"Prestwick, Scotland, Captain Darling, that's home, via Gander, Newfoundland, for fuel."

"Yes, Captain Zola."

"Was that a Zola with a capital 'Z' or a Xola with a capital 'X'?"

"When I click my heels to my new superior officer it's the Zola with the 'Z', but when we kiss it's the Xola wolf with the brown-black eyes."

"The Xola wolf from the Masai Mara," she said happily. "We've got wolves there too."

"Well, let's get cracking, time to get the hell out of here." I could not remain in my chair any longer, anxious to leave.

"Yes, Jack, let's go home together; to *our* home."

"Do you know why I shouted my name, when they winched me up into the helicopter in the boson's chair? Just one word, just my name, 'Zola' was all that crossed my lips. I was afraid that you would not hear it and if you did not know my name you could not fall in love with me. It's true, isn't it? A man cannot fall in love with a woman unless he knows her name."

We were on finals into Gander, Newfoundland, for our fuel stop and I thought this must be the perfect moment for a soul-searching conversation. But I enjoyed it – it gave me a beautiful feeling of warmth and affection.

"There could be an element of truth in that." I suggested.

"Oh, don't be so blasé, element of truth! It is the absolute truth. I was on fire from the moment you wrestled me into the survival suit in that dark and half flooded deckhouse, ten minutes away from drowning. You had stepped into my life as the man who instantaneously captured my heart and soul, on the spot, then and there – forever. By the time the boson's chair had come down for me I knew that my fate was sealed: I loved you then and I love you now and as long as fate will let me. Did I commit a crime by catching you, setting a trap by throwing my name at you and now coming to cast a spell on you in the flesh? Speak up, mystery man!"

". . . yeah, some crime, for which we'll both get life."

". . . and a day, together in paradise, if fate will let us."

"Well, dearest Zola, I've got something for you too: I'll have you booked on conspiracy charges, together with your accomplices, one wolf named Xola and my fantasy dream-woman named Carla Cheung."

"Do I have to be jealous of them?"

"That depends, I don't quite know how to define your relationship."

"What is there that you don't know, tell me . . . why?"

"The three of you are one."

The Author

After about forty years of working in America, Europe and Africa, first as a consulting engineer and then in aviation, H John Grube decided that there were other sides to life, like sailing around the world and writing books. After many interesting and demanding projects he said good-bye to engineering and aviation and has since developed a keen interest in environmental issues, believing that our world is a place worth saving, as it is the only one we've got. As the father of three grown-up children he firmly believes that we owe a debt of care and diligence to posterity and tries to live up to that wherever possible.

He hails from the grater Baltic Region that comprised Estonia, Latvia, Lithuania and East Prussia, the same part of the world as Jacob Gershovitz and Israel Baline, better known as George Gershwin and Irving Berlin. He shares his birthplace Koenigsberg with philosopher Immanuel Kant and witnessed the dying days of Nazi Germany, leaving his native East Prussia in April 1945 across the Baltic Sea in the last ship to make it out of Pillau, the last remaining sea port in the Eastern Baltic Sea, then still in German hands, moments ahead of the advancing Red Army. He later came to attend high school in Santa Barbara, CA, USA, studied engineering in America, Germany and the Netherlands and spent the greater part of his working life in the United States, the United Kingdom and eastern and central Africa.

H John Grube press twenty-one is

Hans-Jochen Grube author and publisher
press twenty-one
Cologne/Koeln, Germany

H John Grube press twenty-one is

Hans-Jochen Grube author and publisher
press twenty-one
Cologne/Koeln, Germany

www.ingramcontent.com/pod-product-compliance
Lightning Source LLC
LaVergne TN
LVHW091242190726
843491LV00001B/104

* 9 7 8 3 9 8 1 7 4 1 9 7 1 *